CASTLES

Rosie Serdiville & John Sadler

D1052652

CASEMATE

Oxford & Philadelphia

Published in Great Britain and
the United States of America in 2018 by
CASEMATE PUBLISHERS
The Old Music Hall, 106–108 Cowley Road, Oxford OX4 1JE, UK
1950 Lawrence Road, Havertown, PA 19083, USA

© Casemate Publishers 2018

Paperback Edition: ISBN 978-1-61200-613-0
Digital Edition: ISBN 978-1-61200-614-7 (epub)

A CIP record for this book is available from the British Library

Printed in the Czech Republic by FINIDR, s.r.o.

Typeset in India by Versatile PreMedia Services. www.versatilepremedia.com

For a complete list of Casemate titles, please contact:

CASEMATE PUBLISHERS (UK)
Telephone (01865) 241249
Email: casemate-uk@casematepublishers.co.uk
www.casematepublishers.co.uk

CASEMATE PUBLISHERS (US)
Telephone (610) 853-9131
Fax (610) 853-9146
Email: casemate@casematepublishers.com
www.casematepublishers.com

Dedicated to Leo, Helen and Henry. For use when building castles in the air

'Castle: a large fortified building or group of buildings; a stronghold: a formerly fortified mansion'

Concise Oxford Dictionary

'To the left, and lying in the distance, might be seen other towers and battlements; and divided from the town by a piece of artificial water, which extended almost around it, arose the Dangerous Castle of Douglas.
Sternly was it fortified, after the fashion of the Middle Ages, with donjon and battlements; displaying, above others, the tall tower which bore the name of Lord Henry's or the Clifford's Tower.'

Sir Walter Scott, *Castle Dangerous*

CONTENTS

INTRODUCTION

FORTRESS – GUARDIANS OF THE REALM

Spend some time in newcastle's laing art gallery, a magnificent Victorian building crammed with images of the North of England, real and imagined. Here, marvel at John Martin's epic canvases, one of which shows a Welsh bard, a Victorian hippie, shaking a defiant if useless fist at an armoured column of English knights toiling towards a massive mountain-top citadel, as aloof as the clouds, Olympian and brooding. Great rousing stuff it is, fodder for the imagination of any small child. Castles, medieval donjons, all of them still to be found in any toy shop. Plus the new incarnations, the homes of fantasy, the lodges of the mythical warrior and the sorcerer. It's no accident that the author of the *Game of Thrones* found inspiration wandering Hadrian's Wall and the bastles and castles that surround it.

The question is, 'what is a castle?' Pretty obvious you'd think, the country is dotted with them, but historians have recently been struggling with an exact definition. Looking at what the dictionary has to say (above) it seems clear enough. Marc Morris (see bibliography) quotes from the great Professor Brown in his seminal *English Castles* who stresses the residential nature of the castle, 'fortified residence or a residential fortress'. A castle may be different to a fort or fortress in that the essence of it is somebody lives there, however it is more than a country house with attitude, the purpose of the building has its impact on the wider landscape.

Castles live on in the mind, long centuries after they had any real fighting purpose. The Victorians were falling over themselves to add a dash of gothic and, where they could afford it, to carry on crenellating. Every year visitors crowd the great British fortresses; Dover, the Tower of London, Arundel, Warwick, Conwy, Caernarvon, Alnwick, Bamburgh, Edinburgh and Stirling. The movies help, from Camelot to Castle Dracula, *Schloss Adler*, High Dunsinane and *Throne of Blood*. Castles are not just a British or European tradition.

Even the better class of fakes bring the visitors in, Castell Coch and Eilean Donan. The archetypal Scottish highland castle, even if it was built in the 1920s, backdrop for numerous movies including perhaps most memorably *Highlander* with Christopher Lambert and Sean Connery, a brilliant fantasy film with a make-believe castle. Several other Scottish castles, notably Doune, have done very well out of big-budget TV dramas such as *Outlander* or *Game of Thrones*. Neither of these is history entire, but the castles look good, they're in the mould for myth which is probably why we still love them so much.

Today we can look around: when these places were lordly dwellings only those sufficiently high up the feudal pyramid would have access, and even then the lord's private quarters would have been strictly out of bounds. Time and the heritage industry have democratised the castle.

Eilean Donan Castle, Scotland. (Syxaxis Photography, Wikimedia Commons, CC BY-SA 4.0)

Model of Harbottle Castle c. 1500. (Author's own, courtesy of Adam Barr (Adamski))

Recently, having (thanks to Heritage Lottery Fund and Northumberland National Park), completed a scale model of Harbottle Castle in Upper Coquetdale as it might have looked *c.* 1500, we had several comments from visitors: 'Is that it? Doesn't seem much'. They could have said it doesn't look much like the movies and they would have been right. But that's the way it actually was. Hollywood raised the bar way above history. The real thing was altogether more business-like, squatter, scruffier and frequently knocked about. The men and women who built them weren't thinking of their tourist heritage: they wanted to stay alive and in charge. By and large they succeeded.

Harbottle, like most, isn't the product of a single burst of building development. In part, castles, which so dominated the British landscape for several centuries, are organic. They grew and changed as trends shifted; becoming increasingly sophisticated through the high Middle Ages until, by the early 16th century, guns and gunpowder rendered them largely anachronistic. Norham, that great 'Queen of Border Fortresses' in North Northumberland resisted a Scots siege for two years, 1318–20. In 1513, however, James IV's mighty artillery brought the place down in under a week. This was a very loud form of redundancy notice.

The motte and bailey defences of Launceston Castle in England. (Chris Shaw, Wikimedia Commons, CC BY-SA 2.0)

Warfare was for centuries dominated by the perpetual and symbiotic duel between those who tried to erect defences and those who wanted to knock them down. The age of gunpowder fatally altered the balance. Prior to that, the advantage typically lay with the defender.

It was the Normans, with their timber motte and bailey fortifications, who truly introduced the castle into England (though some now debate this). During the 12th century, timber was gradually replaced by masonry; great stone keeps such as Rochester, Orford, Conisburgh, Richmond and Newcastle, soared impressively. The late, great George Macdonald Fraser once described grim Hermitage in Liddesdale as 'sod off in Stone'. That's about right.

The castle was not just a fort; it was the lord's residence, the seat and symbol of his power, centre of his administration, a secure base from which his mailed household could hold down a swathe of territory. Castles were both potent and symbolic. The dire civil wars of Stephen and Matilda spawned a pestilence of unlicensed building, fuelling a magnatial threat to crown authority. Castles grew thickest on the disputed marches of England, facing the Welsh and Scots. In the north-west the mighty red sandstone fortress of Carlisle rose up, a clear warning to those living north of the border who coveted Cumberland.

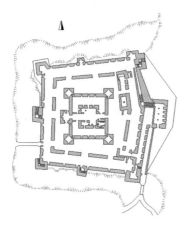

Plan of the concentric crusader castle at Belvoir in Israel. (Wikimedia Commons, CC BY-SA 3.0)

Concentric crusader castle at Krac des Chevaliers in Syria. (Guillaume Rey, from Guillaume Rey: Étude sur les monuments de l'architecture militaire des croisés en Syrie et dans l'île de Chypre *(1871), Wikimedia Commons)*

Concentric castles, influenced by Arab and Byzantine precedent, appeared when Edward I began constructing his great chain of towering Welsh fortresses. This was policy in stone, a

Aerial view of Belvoir. (צ.אסף at Hebrew Wikipedia – Transferred from he.wikipedia to Commons by teqoah., Public Domain)

ring around the Welsh mountains just in case anybody forgot who was really boss. Elsewhere, as the country enjoyed a long spell of peace, many lords invested in what might now be termed 'makeovers'. Their aim? To improve standards of living rather than add defences. Larger, more ornate chapels and fine, great halls replaced their workaday predecessors. Gardens and orchards were laid out to provide tranquil spaces within the walls.

Most castles of the pre-concentric era period relied upon the strength of the great keep. Tall, massive, towering in fine ashlar with the lower vaulted basement reserved for storage and an entrance at first-floor level, they are now frequently enclosed in a defensive fore-building. On this level we would typically find the great hall with the chapel and the lord's private apartment or solar on the second floor above. Spirals were set in the thickness of the wall leading to a rooftop parapet walk, often with corner towers. A strong stone wall enclosed the bailey, which would also house the domestic facilities. The keep was essentially a refuge, a passive defence. The space was easy to defend and with only a handful of soldiers, properly supplied, the keep could hold out for a long time.

Orford Castle with surrounding earthworks. (Gernot Keller, Wikimedia Commons, CC BY-SA 2.5)

From the reign of Henry II onward, strong flanking towers were frequently added to provide a defence against mining. The polygonal keep at Orford in Suffolk (1165–73) is a fine example. At Pembroke, William the Marshal built an entirely circular keep. The curtain wall was also raised and strengthened, furnished with D-shaped towers, the section beyond the curtain rounded at the corners to frustrate mining. These towers made the attacker's job far more difficult. If they breached or surmounted a section of the rampart, they'd be corralled between the towers which would, in turn, have to be assaulted. This paved the way for a fully concentric design where the strength of the whole was distributed through the towers. The great keep, as a single defensive feature, became far less important.

Traditional timber-framed siege engines, unchanged from classical times – the ballista and the mangonel – dominated warfare during the 12th and 13th centuries – cannon and the Devil's Roar were yet to make their appearance. The ballista was, in effect, a giant crossbow which hurled a bolt or occasionally stones at the enemy's walls. It was intended as an anti-personnel weapon, flensing unwary defenders from the parapet. It was used to provide covering 'fire' for an assault. Though we can't really talk about 'fire' as none of these wooden weapons did actually fire, there was no black powder charge or spark involved; more correctly we use the term 'shooting' (as with a bow).

Chief among engines was the mighty trebuchet. Most probably Arab in origin, this worked by counterpoise – the device was built with a timber beam pivoted between two sturdy posts. One end of the beam had ropes affixed and the sling was fitted to the other. Initially, when the ball was loaded into the sling, a group of hefty infantry simply hauled on the ropes, dragging upwards the shorter end of the timber. The sling, at the 'ready' moment, released the projectile.

Latterly, a large counterweight, a timber-framed box casing, filled with soil or rubble supplanted raw muscle. The machines were far larger – the box might weigh over 4,536 kg (10,000lb). These trebuchets consumed vast quantities of timber in their building. Missiles, which might weight 45–90 kg (100–200 lb) or even more, were flung at a high trajectory, like the shell from a later howitzer. The internal spaces of the castle could be deluged in a rain of stones that, shattering on impact, would send lethal shards whizzing like shrapnel. The bombardment came to resemble an artillery barrage, deadly and relentless, the defenders forced to seek shelter while it lasted.

When the commander, lord or 'castellan' became aware that an attack was imminent (good scouting and intelligence were vital), it was time to prepare. Supply was a major concern. Clearly, adequate quantities of food and a clean water supply were essential to maintain the garrison for what might stretch to several months of encirclement. Sheep, cattle and livestock would be gathered in, the surrounding countryside stripped.

Ditches would be cleared and consolidated; repairs to masonry undertaken, trees, bushes and inconvenient settlements demolished, 'slighted' to deny an enemy any cover. Timber hoardings, called 'brattices', would be erected over the parapet walk to provide a covered fighting platform, the defenders' own artillery serviced and repaired, supplies of missiles and arrows stockpiled.

Siege warfare was costly, time consuming and tedious. An attacker might be stuck in front of the walls for long and frustrating weeks, consuming his own stores at a rapid rate, at risk from the defenders' counter-attacks or sallies, from dysentery in the crowded lines or from a relieving force. He would try to negotiate; to persuade the castellan to come to terms. If the commander just gave up before the siege lines were fixed then convention would allow him and his defenders to march out under arms and depart unmolested (in theory anyway).

If negotiations failed, threats might prevail. Prisoners were useful bargaining chips. In 1139 King Stephen persuaded the mother of Roger le Poer to surrender Devizes or see her son hanged before the walls. Edward III, in 1333, when recovering Berwick, threatened to hang the governor's two young sons if the place didn't open its gates. The stubborn Scot refused and had to endure the agony of watching his boys die.

As any siege dragged on, the quantum of mercy shrank accordingly. If the place was vanquished by storm then the attackers were free to kill everyone. An offer of clemency, once extended, might not be repeated. Where the defenders, finding themselves in dire straits, asked for terms they might find the besieger less amenable than at the start of the blockade. Even when a commander was disposed to be reasonable, his men, eager for loot, might just not listen. King Edward Longshanks, as the English took Berwick upon Tweed in 1296, was horrified at the atrocities his own soldiers inflicted.

Civil war was always going to be worse. While kings and magnates would not wish to see domestic towns and castles sacked, private grudges were too often played out. The storming of Beziers in July 1209 during the suppression of the Cathars was notorious: the whiff of heresy was sufficient for French knights to slaughter heretics and believers alike. The Papal legate, Arnaud Almaric, is said to have quipped – 'Kill them all. God will know his own'. After the battle of Hexham in Northumberland in May 1464, more Lancastrians were executed in the clear-up operation than had probably died in the fight.

Morale was a vital factor, loss of nerve on the defenders' part, or the effects of exhaustion and despair, could swiftly erode any garrison's will to resist. When laying siege to Stirling in 1304 Longshanks refused to allow the defenders to formally surrender. The king had his engineers build a giant trebuchet, the 'War Wolf' and he was anxious to test its effect. He had even erected stands so ladies of the court could enjoy the sport.

Siege warfare was both attritional and infinitely brutal. Henry V, in the 15th century, like Julius Caesar before him, refused to allow French civilians, expelled by the garrison commanders as *bouches inutiles* ('useless mouths') to pass through the lines. They became trapped in a bleak no-man's-land, left to squat there in filth and famine while the siege continued. Disease was a spectre that stalked both sides, especially during hot summer weather, yet it was extremely difficult to maintain a siege during stark, freezing winter.

In terms of tactics, storming or 'escalade' was the quickest method of subduing a garrison but very risky, the attacker might easily sustain significant losses. Such instances were relatively rare and it was far more common for the aggressor just to starve the garrison out. This entailed less tactical risk but was inevitably much lengthier.

The besieger had both to plan and fortify his camp, stockpile his supplies, provide tents or bothies for his men and attempt some basic form of sanitation. To be effective the blockade had to seal the besieged off completely. When throwing his great ring of concentric castles around the conquered principality of Wales, Edward I sited these so that, in the main, they could be re-supplied from the sea. Re-victualled defenders made a besiegers' task more difficult.

Surprise and subterfuge were naturally at a premium. After the death of Edward I his son and successor lacked the necessary fire and fury to maintain his father's war against Bruce in Scotland. King Robert steadily clawed back the vital outposts, several of which were won by coup de main as the Scots lacked both the resources and engineering skills demanded of a conventional besieger. Treachery saved time and effort. If the attacker could cultivate or bribe a faction within the walls; create some form of Trojan horse, then a cash investment, *geltkrieg,* might pay dividends.

To conduct a full-scale siege of an enemy stronghold was likely to be a long-term, largely static affair, tying down the attacker's army or certainly large portions of it and robbing him of any strategic initiative. Conversely, simply bypassing the enemy stronghold was to leave a potential threat behind. As an alternative, the fortress could be masked by sufficient forces to neutralise the defenders whilst the main attacking force remained active in the field.

'Frightfulness', what we'd now call terror, was another tactic available to the attacker. He could intimidate the castellan into surrender by wreaking havoc across his lands. In 1123 Henry I 'took up' all the space around Pont-Audemer for a good 20 miles or so. Contemporary writers confirm that the army's scouts or 'prickers' also functioned as incendiaries and foragers, seizing what the army might use, destroying the rest. These tactics were limited during civil wars, what king wishes to waste his own lands? His quarrel is generally with an individual lord or magnate rather than their wider following or affinity. Penniless subjects pay no taxes.

When the attacking general decided to storm the place, he would send in his assault troops; chosen men, who would attempt to set ladders against the walls. Archers, protected by timber hoardings or pavises, would unleash a missile storm intended to keep the defenders' heads down. The castellan's men would rely on their own bows and on a range of missiles to smash the ladders, massing to deal with those who managed to get a foothold. All very desperate and messy. If a castle was protected by a moat that frustrated attempts at mining then the attacker might have a go with a ram or screw, manoeuvred over the moat on a pontoon of fascines (bundles of sticks).

The ram would be a solid baulk of timber housed in a wheeled shed to offer the crew some protection. The beam was slung on ropes from the roof, then swung to and fro to gather momentum. A screw was used to bore rather than batter. Defenders would lower large hooks to catch and fling the contraption aside or drop great boulders in an attempt to smash the protective carapace and crush its occupants.

A siege tower or 'belfry' was a movable, timber structure higher at its upper level than the wall and providing a platform for archers while infantry charged across a drawbridge. Like all wooden devices these monsters were difficult to move, vulnerable to fire and required a great deal of effort to construct. Protracted siege warfare stripped the land around of raw materials as well as produce – worse than any plague of locusts. Even if the attacker finally gave up and moved on, he'd inevitably leave a desert behind.

Mining has an ancient provenance – the first mention occurs in the bible (Joshua before the great walls of Jericho). It was a difficult and, for the miner, dangerous business. A shaft was sunk to a corner of the wall or tower with a chamber excavated directly underneath. This was supported by timber props, the whole space crammed with combustible material and then fired to collapse a section of masonry.

Naturally, military architects would endeavour to frustrate the miners' efforts by siting the castle on a foundation of solid rock or by providing water defences. The base of the wall could be splayed or 'battered' to provide a more formidable obstacle. The miner had to conceal the entrance to his shaft to avoid alerting the defenders; dead ground or buildings could provide ideal cover. As an alternative to bringing down a section of wall the shaft could continue into the bailey to allow a storming party of attackers to launch a surprise attack and seize the gates. Edward III used a network of old tunnels under Nottingham castle to mount a successful coup against his mother and Roger Mortimer.

A prudent castellan might place buckets of water on the parapet to detect tremors. If the wall was breached then the defenders could attempt to plug the gap with timbers or construct temporary screen walls. The more enterprising, on detecting intimations of mining, might attempt to sink a countermine. The objective was to break into the attackers' shaft and engage his miners in a desperate and savage subterranean melee.

Castles, as we identified earlier, weren't just fortresses. Many never saw hostile action in their entire history. They combined several key functions within the feudal hierarchy. They were a residence for the lord, his family and retainers, also centres for his wider and all-important network of dependents and allies, his 'affinity'. They were certainly bastions but as much for offence as defence. Control of territory was what it was all about. Harbottle Castle, as we'll see (chapter 4), is a perfect example.

The castle also functioned as an administrative and judicial centre, the hub of surrounding communities, a place where justice was dispensed. All of this went to reinforce the lord's status and 'good lordship' was a central pillar of feudalism. It was his duty not just to rule his people but to offer them stability and security. A strong castle facilitated all of this.

In many ways the development of castles in England mirrors the process which occurred in Europe. In part but not completely, certainly the great tower or donjon is a feature of many French and German castles but, further east into the vestiges of the Eastern Empire, the tattered rump of Rome's imperial glory, designs varied. The Byzantines were the inheritors of Roman military technology, codified by Vegetius in the 4th century AD. If we look at say, the magnificent Theodosian walls of Istanbul (4th–5th century AD), we can see the layout is concentric, strength spread rather than concentrated. It would not be until the Crusades that these influences would permeate into northern Europe.

European knights didn't just seek crusading glory in the Holy Land, they marched east into what is now Saxony and the Baltic states, taking their castles with them. The Teutonic knights would stud their conquered territories with fortresses, initially in timber, rebuilt, often magnificently, in stone. These did their job for several centuries delaying the long twilight of the order's fatal decline until after the disaster at Tannenburg in 1410.

Once gunpowder began knocking down medieval walls with fearful ease, European fortress builders developed the artillery fort, a process that reached its zenith in the career of the greatest master of them all, Sebastien le Prestre de Vauban (1633–1707). His grand designs changed the face of European architecture, especially on the embattled northern borders of France and the emerging Low Countries. History has failed to produce any fortress builder who worked either on such an epic scale or with a more pronounced genius than Vauban. He created a chain of fortified cities that defied that other great genius of the age, John Churchill Duke of Marlborough. His mighty citadel in Lille remains a NATO HQ.

Britain was fortunate in that, after 1066, England at least was never invaded. Wales and Scotland and indeed Ireland were indeed invaded but by England and the disputed marches of the frontier provided a unique environment and savage legacy that isn't echoed anywhere in Europe. Nonetheless both the English and the French constructed fortified townships or 'bastides' along their disputed borders in Langeudoc, Gascony and Aquitaine. There are somewhere between 500 and 700 of these, all built on a similar plan: a central square with grid pattern streets, church and strong walls. Many survive including such beauties as Montpazier, Cordes and Montflanquin.

From an earlier era in south-west France are the seemingly impregnable hilltop forts. They featured in the brutal and protracted 'crusade' against the Cathar heretics of Languedoc. Of these Montsegur in the Ariege (built in the 13th century) and site of the Cathars' last stand, is the most famous. It perches like a stone eagle high on impossible bluffs, it almost defies the imagination how you could build such a place, never mind successfully lay siege to it. Carcassonne in the Aude is a magnificent fortified town, medieval at its core but heavily restored by Viollet-le-Duc in the mid-19th century.

Sir Guy of Dunstanburgh

Sir Guy had just returned from the Crusades, a lonely mailed pilgrim on an empty Northumbrian shore. As he trotted along the coastal plain the skies began to darken and it wasn't long before the first drops of rain were driven against his surcoat by the wind's stiff buffet. As the grey walls of the silent castle rose above him, he thought of shelter to be had, but the dark arrow slits stared blankly, no coloured pennons fluttered proudly, no billowing plumes of smoke spoke of warm fires in the hearths.

He tied his horse to a bent yew tree by the castle drawbridge and stamped over the echoing planks, the wind's wild dirge reverberating beneath the hollow arch. The storm now raged furiously, torrents of rain lashed the stone walls; the savage glare of lightning lit a glowering sky. Suddenly, without warning, a bolt struck through the archway, smashing against the barred gates and bursting their locks. The smashed timbers sagged inward, and the knight, the white-hot sear of the lightning's heat still smouldering, peered in.

The courtyard seemed utterly deserted, forbiddingly so. But knights are not frightened of shadows and he advanced boldly. Another sudden fork of lightning flashed and, as it lit the dark recesses, a shadowy figure stepped out. Totally bald but with a flaming beard this apparition was dressed in a shapeless robe, adorned with curious symbols. A chain with a red-hot brand circled his waist. Might this be a wizard?

Sir Guy was not the type of fellow to be cowed by such a figure, however frightening. Politely, he enquired if he could be of service. 'Indeed yes', replied his host, 'You're the very man I need. I see you are a knight and a brave one too. Nearby is a maiden in terrible distress and in urgent need of rescue, can you assist?'

'Lead on', replied Sir Guy, 'I'm the very man you seek'.

Together, this unlikely pair crossed the empty courtyard; the knight's mailed soles ringing on wet flags, the Bearded One gliding silent as a cat. Now they ascended a flight of steps leading into the dark mass of the great keep itself. The storm was still beating against the walls, but the thick masonry deadened any sound. But there were other noises, strange, half-heard murmurings that seemed to float in the cold air – distant tolling of an unseen bell. This ascent seemed to go on forever, the spiral wound and twisted so that the knight was completely disorientated. His bizarre guide never uttered a single word, the uncertain flickering of his torch cast fitful shadows.

After what seemed an age the pair reached a heavy brass-studded door. A fearsome serpent wound around the bolt, hissing defiance, the light playing over its glossy coils. With a sweep of his burning brand the wizard brushed the snake off and drew back the creaking bolts. The great door swung open and Sir Guy walked through.

He was not prepared for the sheer size of the hall into which he stumbled, the whole vast space tiled in black-and-white marble squares. Ranged around the walls were a hundred fully armed and mounted soldiers, frozen in some timeless magic. At the far end stood a pair of skeletal sentinels, one grasping a hefty double-handed sword, the other a rich hunting horn fabulously studded with ornate gold and jewels. These two grim markers were on either side of a simple wooden coffin, in which lay the most beautiful maiden the knight had ever seen. In an instant his heart was captured but she was enchanted, wrapped up in that same dark alchemy.

Sir Guy was told that if he wanted to free the lady from confinement he'd have to seize either the great sword or the wondrous horn – but on no account must he let go of the prize or drop it until she was fully free. At first the knight was inclined to seize the gleaming blade but some instinct prompted him to try for the horn instead. Raising this to his lips he let out a rich clarion that echoed around the silent hall. Like a rallying cry; the blast seemed immediately to galvanise the still figures of the hundred men at arms who, with sudden violent animation, turned in blind fury upon Sir Guy.

Instinctively he drew his sword, and as he did so he dropped the horn! In that whirling instant his vision dimmed and found himself mysteriously transported back to the stunted yew tree beyond the walls of the castle, where his horse was still tethered, waiting patiently. Search as he might he never saw the wizard, the enchanted hall or the sleeping maiden again.

They say he's searching still. So, if on a wild and windy day you should spot a solitary horseman down by the shore, bent against the cold north wind, remember Sir Guy.

The legend of Dunstanburgh Castle on the Northumbrian Coast is retold in the 'Minstrelsy' and in other sources.

TIMELINE

1066	Battle of Hastings; the beginnings of motte and bailey.
1139–53	Wars of Stephen and Matilda.
1216	Siege of Rochester Castle.
1216	Siege of Dover Castle.
1265	Siege of Kenilworth Castle.
1277–83	Welsh Wars of Edward I.
1283	Harlech Castle built.
1283	Caernarfon Castle built, though left partly unfinished.
1289	Conwy Castle built.
1290	Caerphilly Castle built.
1295	Beaumaris Castle constructed, though not finished.
1296	Siege and storm of Berwick; beginning of Scottish Wars of Independence.
1304	Great Siege of Stirling Castle.
1306	Siege of Kildrummy Castle.
1455	Siege of Threave Castle.
1455–87	Wars of the Roses.
1464	Siege of Bamburgh Castle.
1513	Siege of Norham Castle.
1642–46	First Civil War.
1644	Siege of Newcastle.

TECHNICAL GLOSSARY

Allure — Fighting platform of the parapet – the wall walk.

Ballista — Form of catapult, dating from the classical era, shooting a missile from an integral bow, tensioned by the operation of a windlass.

Bailey — Castle courtyard enclosed by a wall.

Barbican — An outwork, constructed so as to provide protection for a castle or the fortified gateway of a town. This could be erected in stone (permanent) or in timber as a temporary additional defence.

Bastion — An external extension of the main castle wall offering a wider angle of defence, also called a bulwark.

Belfry — A wooden siege tower, moved forward against the enemy's walls on wheels or rollers.

Bill — A polearm, born of the union of the agricultural tool with the military spear to create a formidable hafted weapon.

Blazon — The formal description of a coat of arms or banner.

Bolt — A short, thick arrow or quarrel, shot from a crossbow.

Bracer — Plate defences for the lower arms.

Brattice — A form of timber hoarding built onto the parapet of a castle and corbelled out

	on wooden beams, provided a protected shooting gallery for the defenders' bows.
Brigandine	A protective, flexible doublet with horn or metal plates sewn in.
Broadsword	A double-edged, generally single-handed knight's sword.
Buckler	A small round shield or target used for parrying an opponent's weapon and delivering fast beats or punches.
Captain	The officer in charge of a particular location, whose authority was limited to that place and did not extend beyond.
Chateau	French term for a lord's castle or residence.
Chevauchee	A large spoiling raid into enemy territory, a form of economic warfare.
Conroi	A mounted detachment.
Crenellation (Or castellation)	The castle battlements along the parapet walk; licence to crenellate being in effect the requisite planning permission to construct a castle.
Curtain wall	The outer stone circuit enclosing the castle.
Embrasure	A splayed opening set into the wall of keep or tower for window openings.
Enceinte	The circuit of a defensible place.
Escalade	An assault aimed at storming defences.
Fief	The feudal landholding.
Forebuilding	An extension or addition to the basic keep providing cover for the entrance.
Harness	A full armour of plate, mail or both combined Hauberk a mail shirt, reaching to the knee the Habergeon being the shorter version.
Helm	13th-century great helm worn by knights.
Hide	A measure of land, not consistent but generally around 120 acres.
Jack	A utility form of brigandine, the garment stuffed with rags or tallow.
Lance	A tactical unit of varying size, built up around a knightly retinue.
Leaguer	A siege or blockade.

Mangonel	An engine from throwing stones of classical provenance.
Melee	Contact between large forces, mounted or on foot.
Merlons	The actual battlements, i.e. raised sections of the parapet.
Mesnie	A household knight, of the lord's estate or 'demesne'.
Motte and bailey	A form of Norman timber castle.
Palfrey	An everyday horse.
Pennon or pennant	One of the principal types of medieval flags (from the Latin 'penna' i.e. 'wing' or 'feather'.
Postern	A small gateway ancillary to the main entrance.
Pricker	Scout or skirmisher.
Ravelin	A form of detached outwork designed to split an attacking force and shield the main walls.
Sally port	A form of small postern gate used by a garrison to mount sporadic attacks on the besieging forces.
Sconce	Small earthwork fort or redoubt placed outside principal defences as an artillery position.
Slighting	Deliberate demolition of defences.
Solar	The lord's private quarters.
Trebuchet	A large siege engine with a heavy throwing arm.

CHAPTER 1

→ → → →

DEATH OF THE FIGHTING MAN – IN TIMBER AND STONE

1066–1400

KING HAROLD NEVER SHOULD HAVE LOOKED UP. The arrow in the eye may well be a myth but there is no doubt he lost the battle, his throne and his life. Not a good day however you look at it. It was once accepted that Britain had no real castles prior to those nasty, greedy Normans storming across the Channel. We assume they brought the idea with them, using their timber fortresses (brought with them, flat pack style), to give them a head start on oppressing the country. The reality is a bit more mixed – there was a form of fortress building before 1066. The materials were mostly timber with some stone but there was no motte and bailey. A ringwork was an early form of enclosure castle; it sat on top of a circular mound, a bit like a flatter kind of motte. Inside a wooden palisade were a range of buildings, possibly with a defended gateway. It was a kind of fortified manor house, maybe lacking the strict military application of the motte.

Fifteen years before the battle of Hastings, a monkish chronicler from Peterborough waxed lyrical. Today, we would describe the style as 'tabloid'. He recounts the building of what sounds very much like a castle by a gang of King Edward the Confessor's Norman cronies, describing it as an outrage. In fact these yobbish Norman interlopers were an outrage in general

Reconstructed wooden keep at Saint-Sylvain-d'Anjou, France. (Julien Chatelain, Wikimedia Commons, CC BY-SA 3.0)

but, as Marc Morris describes in his excellent study, this clearly suggests building activity prior to Hastings.

What is a motte? From the days of Charlemagne onwards, local lords in France and Normandy were building fortified dwellings/ garrison outposts. First would come the digging of a larger outer platform (the bailey) with a much steeper conical mound behind (the motte). Both were surrounded by defensible timber cordons and linked by a flying bridge or stairway. Domestic buildings and offices clustered in the bailey while a strong wooden tower was erected on the motte. The latter was not generally residential. It was a last-ditch redoubt which could be held by the few against the many if the many had already broken into and taken the bailey.

At the same time the castle, as the centre of an estate, was a base from which a lord could hold down his lands with a well-trained mini-squadron of mounted, mailed and well-armed knights. Its very strength proclaimed his status – a highly visible badge of his control. He, his family and retainers lived there, his manorial court was held there, it was where he collected his rents. In terms of pure defence, the motte would be situated to control settlements, guard river crossings and coastal estuaries. They were at once tactical; a means of both offence and defence, and strategic, in that they held down large tracts of land. Simple, relatively cheap yet highly effective, they offered a means of stamping a conqueror's seal over subject territory. And for anyone who proves recalcitrant there was always the option of a spot of harrying.

How were motte and bailey castles actually built? Construction demanded a good and ready supply of timber, ideally oak, in which England abounded at the time of the conquest. Logs were felled and dragged by horse transport onto site where they were split, using wedges, into planking. A decent-sized oak yielded as much as a thousand square feet of cladding. The boards could be dressed down with axes to a smooth finish, something that did not require highly specialised craftsmen – village carpenters were adequate. Internal buildings were timber framed with wattle-and-daub panels, again, an undemanding and familiar technology. Roofing would require slates or timber shingles. Thatch, so easy to fire, was avoided.

While **timber** is very useful, it has a telling number of disadvantages. It's cheap, plentiful, light to work by comparison with stone and quick to build. But it deteriorates very quickly – the life span may be as little as 30 years. Worst of all, it's vulnerable to fire. **Stone** may be fire resistant but it is also more expensive, demands highly skilled craftsmen, takes longer and weighs more. When some early timber castles were rebuilt in stone, the ground-works intended to support timber couldn't bear the additional load. Prudhoe in Northumberland is a prime example; the walls slid outwards because the base could not be sufficiently consolidated.

Standards of finish and decoration varied considerably. Some examples depicted on the Bayeux Tapestry indicate high levels of artistic embellishment but this was by no means universal. Motte building was 'statist' only insofar as the king was a guiding force. Each castle was built by an individual lord or knight who was free to exercise his own taste within his means – spartan garrison outpost or luxury gentleman's residence. Baileys were probably more crowded than we might assume from illustrations, which tend to show just a few buildings. A castle might actually have looked more like a fortified village, rammed with jostling interior structures. Even the motte itself, origin of the shell-keep, possibly had a number of buildings crowded behind its palisade.

Castles were located with a purpose. That inevitably meant strategic priorities took precedence over existing civilian settlements. We know that at Cambridge 27 homes were flattened to clear the ground and substantially more at Lincoln. Marc Morris has looked at William of Poitiers' claim that the Conqueror, having subdued Dover, re-fortified the place, throwing up new defences in just eight days. Ingeniously, Morris looks at Victorian pioneer statistics which show a sapper was expected to shift 15 cubic feet of earth per hour (0.75m^3), or 80 cubic feet (4.0 m^3) in a day. As a typical motte required 10,000 cubic metres of earth (22,000 tonnes) to be shifted and packed, it would need five hundred navvies to get the job done in just over a week. One can imagine Duke William was in a good position to summon such a workforce.

All the choicest fiefs in the south went to those closest to William and those who had stood beneath his banners by Senlac Hill. Those less well connected or who turned up after the show didn't do as well and few were that keen on heading north. The king appointed Robert Fitz Richard as castellan at York (building a motte where Clifford's tower now stands). Robert de Comines pushed further north to Durham. These Normans were pretty rough even by local standards and began with a looting spree. The locals took exception and struck back in an untidy running

Image from the Bayeux Tapestry showing William with his half-brothers. William is in the centre, Odo is on the left with empty hands, and Robert is on the right with a sword in his hand. (Wikimedia Commons)

fight. De Comines and his survivors barricaded the Episcopal House but were subsequently burnt alive.

York was next. Fitz Richard was cut down in ambush and what was left of the garrison besieged in their new motte. Relief proved tricky, the Normans oddly timorous. It took William's personal intervention to stem the rot and re-establish royal authority. He reinforced the defences, increased the number of knights and appointed William Fitz Osbern to lead. This replacement had learnt nothing however and continued a reign of terror. In autumn 1069, King Swein of Denmark supported the rebels with a fleet and force of assorted mercenaries. This tipped the odds again and the Normans in York were defeated in a fiery finale.

A medieval form of planning consent, a **licence to crenellate**, was needed to fortify, or 'crenellate' i.e. add battlements, to a structure and make it a fort. This system persisted from the 12th century or possibly earlier to the 16th century. The Civil Wars of Stephen and Matilda had witnessed a whole slew of illegal castles chucked up by feuding barons. Most applicants were drawn from the gentry rather than magnatial class and quite a few licences were issued to women. For a dispute over licensing, see Chapter 4.

By now King William had had quite enough of his troublesome northern subjects. He paid the Danegeld and bought the Scandinavians off. This might have been dangerous but they never came back and he sorted out the locals with a policy of fire and sword. The Harrying of the North was an exercise in terror of biblical proportions, 'He created a desert and called it peace.'

The Bigod Earls of Norfolk joined the dissenting magnates in Stephen's unhappy reign. Henry II confiscated four of the then earl's fortresses and decided to build a new one: a demonstration of centralised power.

Orford, which was constructed between the years 1165 and 1173, is both remarkable and unique. It rises like some mythical enchanted tower, alone on its isolated shore and 12 miles (20 km) northeast of Ipswich. It has a circular tower rising 90 feet (27m) from the flat scrubby plain. The symmetry is compromised by three angular clasping towers projected out from the width of the core (49 feet or 15m). Nevertheless, it's a beautiful job with light airy chambers cleverly angled to maximise the morning's glow.

Orford is around two miles (3.2 km) from the sea – the site runs down towards the River Ore. Most of the outworks have gone but it had a curtain wall, studded with four towers, pierced by a single fortified entrance block. There's some debate as to why Henry opted for this particular, idiosyncratic shape. Current thinking is that this was as much a political as a military statement. In fact the design partly compromises the defence and shows byzantine influences. The angular profile and masonry banding are reminiscent of the great Theodosian walls of Constantinople.

We tend to view keeps as just part of a wider defence complex involving the great tower but also a defensible courtyard with a curtain wall, possibly with additional small towers and a fortified gateway. In France the tower is called a donjon (from the Latin 'dominus' or lord). For our purposes the terms 'great tower', 'keep' and 'donjon' are interchangeable. In some instances, such as at Richmond, the tower has formed a later addition to an existing enclosure castle (here, the great tower replaced an earlier gatehouse). Most are square or rectangular but there are cylindrical keeps as well. A circular construction is better proofed against either missiles or mining.

The mighty, imposing 11th-century keep of Conisbrough, just west of Doncaster still soars impressively, rising incongruous from an industrial and suburban landscape. The curtain wall looks like it belongs somewhere else it is both crude and utilitarian. The towering beautifully ashlared keep is an odd one. Circular in plan, it has six projecting polygonal towers, set symmetrically.

Turrets can add strength and also provide additional chambers. Did lords live in their great towers? Possibly they did but not necessarily, that's perhaps what distinguishes the keep from a hall-tower. This was the era when privacy was rarely a consideration in most homes. Those of high status might have had a solar to withdraw to when they needed confidentiality but they might well have slept somewhere far more public.

There are good examples of hall towers at Colchester and Castle Rising in Norfolk. These don't rise above two stories and at 12th-century Colchester the tower sits squarely on the vaulted podium of the Temple of Claudius. A nice piece of flattery for the emperor but it didn't impress Boudicca. It became one of her first, must-destroy targets.

Beautiful Castle Rising went up around 1140 with access through a fore-building then up a rather grand staircase to a first-floor vestibule and then into the great hall, which occupied one flank of the main block. Keeps, like mottes, were not built by the Romans, they are not an exercise in centralised statism so there's no one-size-fits-all, they're individual. They go up according to taste and the depths of the owner's pocket.

A castle isn't necessarily static, many evolve over time. A good example of a modest hall tower is Aydon in Northumberland, dramatically poised over the Cor Burn and close to the market town of Corbridge. This started life as essentially a civilian building but the fury of the border wars (which escalated in 1296) meant successive generations of knights, the De Reymes, had to steadily upgrade their defences, enclosing the courtyard then adding an extended curtain wall and corner tower.

Lordship is a primary function of feudalism but the individual baron or magnate enjoyed a pretty fair measure of autonomy. His castle defined his power and status, it didn't just represent his place in the layer-cake: it *was* his place. Through the medium of castle building he set his seal on territory. He was the agent and conduit of both the king's writ and his own.

When the two diverge, things can go very badly wrong. The Anarchy of Stephen and Matilda lasted a generation; the Wars of the Roses consumed another. When the king as capstone of the feudal pyramid was weak, the whole edifice began to rock. The Anarchy saw a rash of unlicensed baronial castles spring up. The great siege of Kenilworth (see below), was a major mini-campaign of the Second Barons' War.

Keeps somehow define what we think of as the castle. If anything of their architecture tends to linger in the mind, it's the great tower. Literary castle towers fill the imagination; they're an integral part of Arthurian heritage, Tintagel, Camelot, The Green Knight's Castle, the Fisher King's Castle (even Caernarfon). An awful lot of great towers survive; tangible, timeless and mighty: The White Tower, Rochester, Conisbrough, Richmond, Carlisle, Newcastle, Bamburgh and many others.

In the 19th century, **Gothic literature** picked up on the castle theme, the umbilical that leads back to the high medieval. In the 1870s, a generation ahead of Bram Stoker, Sheridan le Fanu wrote his classic novella *Carmella* about a deadly beguiling vampire. It is based on the real-life Countess Mircalla, whose ruined castle of Karnstein broods as a backdrop. The late Ingrid Pitt, queen of screen vampires played a memorable Carmilla in Hammer's 1970s screen version *The Vampire Lovers*. Poe liked castles too but Bram Stoker gave us Castle Dracula: the idea of the tower of evil has not left us since.

American author F. Paul Wilson has produced a successful series beginning with a very Dracula-style tower in *The Keep* (1981). Perhaps the best-known and most read from the 1980s is *The Name of the Rose* by best-selling Italian author Umberto Eco. The brooding presence of the enigmatic library housed in the mysterious and forbidden *aedificium* (a keep that houses only books – and a few surprises) dominates the unnamed monastery and contains the heart of the mystery.

During the exceedingly dark days of spring 1940, with the British Expeditionary Force trapped on the beaches at Dunkirk, the deliverance that would become legendary was planned beneath Dover Castle – Operation *Dynamo*. This was not the first time the great fortress had been 'the key to England'. The site was very probably fortified during the Iron Age and the Roman invaders established a lighthouse there.

Duke William, as his biographer William of Poitiers tells us, passed via Dover on his initial triumphal march:

> Then he marched to Dover, which had been reported impregnable and held by a large force. The English, stricken with fear at his approach had confidence neither in their ramparts nor in the

Barbican and bartizan: With any defended space, the gatehouse is an obvious weak point – the spot most likely to see enemy attempts to break in. To protect this vulnerable approach, it was quite normal to add an outer gate or barbican, linked to the main entrance by a short length of curtain wall. This created an extra barrier for any attacker, reduced the risks of the main gatehouse being captured by surprise and created a rather nasty little killing zone between the two. If an attack seemed imminent, a further timber barbican or 'barrier' could be thrown up to increase the attacker's difficulties. Good examples of barbicans can be seen at Prudhoe in Northumberland, Alnwick and Newcastle. A bartizan is a small turret which projects from keep or tower, completely supported by the castle wall. These provide additional observation and enfilade.

numbers of their troops ... While the inhabitants were preparing to surrender unconditionally, [the Normans], greedy for money, set the castle on fire and the great part of it was soon enveloped in flames... [William then paid for the repair and] having taken possession of the castle, the Duke spent eight days adding new fortifications to it'. The Castle was first built, entirely out of clay. It collapsed to the ground and the clay was then used as the flooring for many of the ground-floor rooms.

Henry II built many of the castles we still see today. His architect Maurice the Engineer constructed both baileys and the great rectangular tower at Dover. This was around 1170 and while emphasis is still placed on the massive keep, the walls show that the move towards a more concentric castle had already begun. This was probably just as well. Under his younger son, King John; these defences were to be tested to the limit.

John has not had a favourable press; there is a good reason for this. He lost most of the Angevin Empire his father had created

King John. (John Cassell (Internet Archive) [Public domain], Wikimedia Commons)

and fell out with his own great lords. They compelled him, in 1215, to sign Magna Carta. He had not the least intention of keeping to his word and civil war inevitably ensued. Within a year the baronial faction was fast losing ground. To bolster their flagging cause they offered Prince Louis of France the throne if he would back them. He did. That May he landed a substantial force in Kent and John retreated rapidly. He was so disliked that many towns were prepared to recognise the Frenchman as a liberator. However some stayed loyal, Nicholaa de la Haye at Lincoln and Hubert de Burgh who held out at Dover.

In the summer of 1216 a very public meeting took place between John and Lincoln's castellan, Lady Nicholaa de la Haye. Lady Nicholaa, who was then a widow in her fifties or sixties, offered him the castle keys and tendered her resignation as castellan. She was, she said 'a woman of great age and had endured many labours and anxieties in the ... castle and was not able to endure such [burdens] any longer'. King John, for his part, had replied 'sweetly' to these protestations, but instructed her to keep the castle. My beloved Nicholaa, I will that you keep the castle as hitherto until I shall order otherwise'.

How much of this was show? It must have been evident that Nicholaa was perfectly capable of holding the castle, but perhaps she and the king felt that some public display was necessary to confirm this to the local landholders. Female or not, Nicholaa was one of John's most loyal and formidable supporters. Further proof of Nicholaa's high esteem in King John's eyes came on 18 October 1216, when she was appointed joint sheriff of Lincolnshire, alongside Philip Mark, one of John's most notorious henchmen. Nicholaa was still sheriff in May 1217, when she doggedly led the defence of Lincoln castle against Louis' forces, not the first time she had kept it safe for John. She held on through throughout the spring of 1217, when she faced a new threat from a rebel army led by the earl of Winchester and the count of Perche.

Nicholaa's personal role attracted contemporary comment. While royalist writers praised Nicholaa for being 'a worthy lady' deserving of God's protection 'in body and soul', the rebels and the French portrayed her as 'a very cunning, bad-hearted and vigorous old woman'. One suspects she would have preferred the latter description.

The appointment of a woman as a sheriff was highly unusual in an age when women usually held secondary roles in public life. It owed a great deal both to her inherited lands and connections, to her family history (the office of castellan had belonged to her father) and to her strong track record of loyal service to King John.

Of course, it was not unusual for women to take on responsibility for managing (and defending) great estates in the absence of their husbands. Her second husband, Gerard de Camville, readily allowed his wife a role in protecting their family's interests. Such was the level of trust between the couple that when Gerard became entangled in a violent dispute between

Lincoln Castle during the siege. (Matthew Paris, from Matthew Paris (1240–1253), Chronica Majora, volume II, folio 51v (55v), OCLC 9980090., Wikimedia Commons)

the royal chancellor and the future King John in 1191 during King Richard I's absence on the Third Crusade, Gerard placed Nicholaa in charge of Lincoln's defence.

While Gerard had assisted the then Prince John in securing the castles of Nottingham and Tickhill, 'Nicholaa, not thinking about anything womanly, defended … [Lincoln] castle manfully' against the chancellor's forces. When King Richard returned to England in 1194, both Gerard and his wife were punished for their disloyalty and effectively forced to buy their way back into royal favour.

After Gerard's death in January 1215, Nicholaa had returned prominently to the fore in public life, securing control of her inheritance as a widow, and reassuming the office of castellan of Lincoln in the midst of the troubles between King John and his barons.

The final years of Nicholaa's life were dominated by a local power struggle with the Earl of Salisbury whose son had married her granddaughter, Idonea, the heiress to Nicholaa's estates. Time and time again, Nicholaa was called upon to defend her home as the earl tried, ultimately unsuccessfully, to wrest control of Lincoln castle from her, first by force and later by offering hostages. Nicholaa saw him off only relinquishing control of the fortress in June 1226 shortly before her death. Salisbury had died three months earlier...

Dover Castle from the air. (Chensiyuan, Wikimedia Commons, CC BY-SA 4.0)

The other hindrance facing Louis in 1216 was the commander of Dover Castle. Hubert de Burgh had form. Two years earlier, he had led an epic defence of Chinon. In 1216, he had 140 men at arms and plenty of auxiliaries behind Dover's walls – nor was he frightened of the French. In July Louis launched a serious bombardment against a stout timber barbican defending the main gate. Stone-throwing engines kept up a steady barrage whilst miners were at work trying to dig under the outer timber palisade. Crossbowmen crowded into a tall siege tower to snipe at defenders.

Finally, the French launched an infantry assault and took the barbican. The next objective was the main gate, built, of course, in stone. Again Louis miners' went to work and actually brought down one of the twin towers. He sent his infantry in again but this time the defenders (who had thrown up improvised barricades) flung them back. Alarmed by his heavy losses the Frenchman settled down to starve the garrison out. The whole place was closely blockaded and Louis promised a grim reckoning for any survivors. De Burgh wasn't impressed. This stalemate lasted till mid-October when a truce was agreed. Though balked at Dover, the French had still netted a whole crop of gains in the south-east.

The cease-fire came into effect on 14 October. John did the most helpful thing he could have done by dying four days after.

Louis called on de Burgh to throw in the towel – who was he fighting for now? The infant King Henry came the response. Louis left a token force to mask Dover and moved his field army. De Burgh didn't waste the opportunity, packing in provisions and carrying out repairs. He had the aid of an effective fifth column of guerrillas led by the enigmatic 'Willikin of the Weald' (a Robin Hood figure who attacked French outposts and communications) whilst English ships at sea played havoc with the French supply lines.

Louis was not done. In May 1217, a year on he came back – with more men plus more and bigger kit. A huge trebuchet 'Malvoisin' (the term literally means 'bad neighbour', very apt) was deployed. The term was originally used to describe a siege castle and first appears in the description of the siege of Bamburgh Castle in 1095. Just over 100 years later it had a new meaning.

The English irregulars beat up Louis' camp, nicking supplies and cutting throats. The besiegers, under threat from land and

Maurice the Engineer 'Ingeniator', like his successor Master James, ranks as one of Britain's great castle builders. His work endures at both Dover and Newcastle. Both have the distinctive fore-building designed to cover the great keep's vulnerable entrance. At Dover he was paid a daily wage equivalent to a knight's fee, even though in social terms he probably was not from that stratum. His career represents a shift towards a new professionalism in castle design. From that time on, the king would employ an architect/builder (one who had probably served his time as a master mason), to ensure his royal fortresses were built fully in accordance with the latest, most up-to-date trends.

Rochester Castle. (John Armagh, Wikimedia Commons)

sea, were close to becoming the besieged. Worse, that serious bruiser, William the Marshal, the boy king's champion, trounced the French at Lincoln. Louis packed his baggage and departed. This time he wouldn't be back. Defeat on land was followed by disaster at sea. Fittingly it was de Burgh's own flagship which led the charge. Dover was safe and this key was not for turning.

King John had not simply waited for a truce. He besieged Rochester Castle in autumn 1216. The king advanced from Dover to London. Though he had previously installed a royal garrison, the castle had been handed to the Archbishop of Canterbury. It was now held by his castellan, tough William de Albini, a rebel. The siege began on 11 October. The king sailed fire-ships against the bridge over the Medway, cutting off access for any relief force. A sally by the garrison was, with some difficulty, beaten back. John then sacked and slighted the cathedral, a signal for Archbishop Langton. Siege engines were constructed and mining operations succeeded in opening a breach in the outer wall. By early November the royalists had taken the bailey.

More mines were sunk under the south-east tower of the great keep. John had foraged requisitioned two dozen pigs who, having fed his army, continued to serve. Their fat was used to fire the timbers supporting the mine-chamber. Down came the tower. Despite this, the rebels still clung to a portion of the keep – the great tower was divided by a strong internal partition that effectively created two defensible zones. Those who surrendered were savagely mutilated to reflect the king's frustration. It was only on 30 November that the ravenous survivors capitulated. The patriotic swine were awarded their own memorial, the garrison were lucky to escape with their lives.

John had won but the siege had left him with a hefty bill – it had cost in the region of £1,000 per day. That was a prodigious outlay to subdue a rebel company of fewer than a hundred men at arms. So, not only were sieges protracted, they entailed a huge drain on the attackers' resources.

Rochester wasn't quite done yet. A Second Barons' War erupted in 1264 when Simon de Montfort rebelled against Henry III. The son was as bad as the father in many ways. This war began as both sides jockeyed for a strategic death grip. For Simon, moving against Rochester could restore the strategic initiative he had earlier mislaid. The king couldn't ignore this threat; possession of Rochester was just too critical all round. He would have to march his army south, away from London and into the belly of baronial territory to lift any siege.

Committing yourself to battle was not the first reflex of any medieval commander. To seize an enemy's strongholds, waste his lands and generally duff up his people were far less hazardous ways of bringing your opponent to his knees. Besides, though this was civil war, there had not yet been any serious killing. Rebel knights taken by the royalists at Northampton had not been mistreated or even sentenced. Both sides were still on the level plain of manoeuvre. The trouble with killing was that blood, once shed, was never easily washed away. A feud begun next year at Evesham between the Despensers and the Mortimers would still be festering into the reign of Edward II.

By 17 April Rochester was under attack. Gilbert de Clare came from the south, his base being at Tonbridge, whilst de Montfort, moving out of London, occupied the banks of the Medway facing the great fortress. Locals proved energetically royalist in sentiment. The bridge was partly demolished (though enough of the structure survived to form an ad hoc barbican jutting into the water.) A number of probes were seen off. But de Montfort sent in fire-ships on the evening of the 18th, and created enough confusion to allow the rebels to break into the town. Next day they captured the outer bailey but, just like last time, the keep held out.

Henry reacted with a burst of energy, hurling his forces south in a series of forced marches, the army covering up to 20 miles a day. By 20 April the royalists were at Grantham; less than a week later at Aylesbury. By dusk on the 26th Henry's mounted vanguard had pressed on an impressive 45 miles to Croydon, just another day's ride from Rochester. De Montfort's trebuchets were in action but making little headway. Henry probably commanded approximately 1,500 cavalry and several thousand infantry, most probably mounted on garrons.

Such a rapid response posed real problems for the rebels. The siege had pulled the royalists south. Now they could choose to shift their axis of advance toward London, leaving the earl stuck before Rochester when his grip on the capital was far from secure. The baronial army had to decide on a suitable course of action. By the 26th their scouts confirmed enemy forces were only 25 miles away, poised to strike. For de Montfort there was no viable alternative but to break up the siege and return to London, he couldn't risk losing the city. Giving up on Rochester meant loss of face but was, still, the lesser of two evils.

The second great siege of Rochester proved a lot less damaging than the first. The Barons' War was generally very traumatic. The king lost a battle, most of his army and his liberty at Lewes. Prince Edward, 'Longshanks' (i.e. 'long legs'), then took over, escaping from house arrest and raising a new royalist army. He beat up rebel quarters at Kenilworth then, after a fast-moving campaign, bottled de Montfort up in Evesham and annihilated his men

Arrow and gun loops: Defending archers could shoot down from towers or parapet but to provide even greater 'firepower', arrow slits were constructed in tower walls. These are narrow apertures with a much wider space or embrasure behind which gave the archer space to load and choose a stance. The chances of any enemy being able to put a retaliatory arrow through the loop were minimal. As time progressed, artillery and hand-held firearms began to replace bows necessitating the creation of gun loops. These came in various shapes but often involved creating a round porthole type feature at the base of the loop allowing a barrel to project.

when they tried to break out. The earl went down fighting and while the battle effectively ended the war, Longshanks was left with a fair amount of mopping up.

Mighty Kenilworth, despite Edward's successful raid, stayed firmly in rebel hands. The subsequent siege would be epic, on the scale of Rochester in the earlier war. The castle had come to de Montfort in 1244. He had strengthened an already formidable set of defences. It was in a naturally strong position, commanding a rocky knoll that rises up from surrounding wetlands. The great red-sandstone fortress dominates the surrounding plain.

King John had originally replaced the timber motte dug by Geoffrey de Clinton with a stone donjon, adding an outer bailey. He also built the strengthened dam or causeway. To the west and south the approach was covered by an expanse of water, the Mere, 20 hectares of it. The outer bailey wall was lengthy, enclosing a substantial area and studded with projecting towers. Inside that an inner ward, even stronger, was dominated by high square towers and an imposing keep.

The water turned the fortress into an island. To the north and beyond the Mere lay a broad moat which lapped around as far

The Great Keep at Kenilworth. (Paul Johnson, Wikimedia Commons, CC BY-SA 3.0)

as the Lower Pool, yet another square-shaped, miniature lake. This shielded the causeway which ran north-westwards from a fortified outwork on the Brays. This too was protected by water. The whole enormous complex, with a garrison of over 1,000 was a besieger's nightmare. Kenilworth would be no pushover.

Longshanks wasn't initially involved in the siege; command and direction was entrusted to his younger brother Edmund. It was a big job and Prince Edmund had mobilised levies from ten counties. They laboured to fell timber and build some truly monster trebuchets, set up in the south-west quadrant, battering away at the Brays while others ringed the north and east.

The siege was long and lively. The defenders kept up an enthusiastic fusillade of abuse while the attackers attempted an amphibious assault across the Mere, drawing landing craft down from Chester; costly and ultimately futile. Nobody was winning but everyone was tired. The king had, largely thanks to his son, clung on to his throne and the rebels had nowhere to go. It was time for a political settlement, bargaining not battling.

Henry of Almain and the papal legate were appointed arbitrators and by, 31 October 1265, they had drafted the Dictum of Kenilworth. The key provision was that all those who had been attainted (stripped of their lands) might buy them back. Prices were fixed on a sliding tariff dependent upon the level of involvement. For those most implicated, including the Kenilworth garrison, this was a rather feeble inducement and did not immediately bring the drawn-out siege to an end. Hunger did: the starving, none too fragrant, survivors finally opened the gates in December. That was pretty much the end of the Second Barons' War.

The Castle of Seven Proud Shields

We all know the Romans built Hadrian's Wall. But what about King Arthur? There's a lot to suggest the once and future king was here too. The wonderfully sited fort of Birdoswald (Camboglanna in Latin) is a contender for the location of Camlann, that final, dim, weird battle in the west. High Rochester in Redesdale is possibly the site of another Round Table punch-up just beyond the old frontier.

Coming from the east, Sewingshields is where the line of the wall begins its majestic rise along the Whin Sill. Long after the Romans left, possibly near the present farm, stood a small medieval castle. According to William Weaver Tomlinson writing in the 1860s, the walls (2.5 metres in places) could still be seen. Today there's no trace, but we know the place existed; records for the 1540s record it being owned by Heron of Chipchase.

Scott uses the place in canto six of *Harold the Dauntless* as the 'Castle of Seven Proud Shields'. The Reverend Hodgson, a noted local antiquary, insisted Arthur, Guinevere and their court were all locked in an eternal enchantment in some deep cavern, just below the castle on its crag. At the entrance, he maintained, stands a marble table carrying the sword of the stone, a garter and bugle. If one is used to cut the other and the instrument blown, the whole ensemble will ride free.

Now, one day the shepherd from Sewingshields had found a seat among the ruins and was doing a spot of darning when he dropped his wool. Oddly, the ball simply seemed to vanish, to slip down between the rocks and heather. Curious, he began to pile some of the stones and found he'd uncovered the blocked-up mouth of an underground passage. Well he just had to have a look. Down he went down and down, a very long tunnel but one with a light at the end. A very small light but he felt drawn towards it, gleam swelling as he felt his cautious way along the smooth clammy surface. This tunnel did have an end – a huge subterranean chamber, so tall he couldn't see the roof, like an underground cathedral. In the centre an everlasting phantom flame threw out weird, eerie light that played over the frozen faces of the legendary king, his queen and serried ranks of knights, flickering over mail and sharpened points. And here was the table with sword, and garter and bugle.

He knew the story so, as if commanded by some unseen power, our farmer drew the fabulous sword, the broad blade marvellously balanced and light in the heft. The keen edge easily sliced the garter and, as though galvanised, the whole company began to stir, a sudden animation from frozen to live that so terrified the shepherd he dropped blade and bugle, then pelted back down the tunnel. In his panic he had omitted to blow the necessary fanfare so, after this first stirring, the whole Round Table sank back into perpetual trance. He never found that entrance ever again – nor has anyone else.

CHAPTER 2

BASTARD FEUDALISM

15TH CENTURY

On the dank late autumn evening of 11 december 1282, Llewellyn ap Gruffadd, leader of a Welsh nation locked in bitter conflict with Edward I, briefly left his army (7,000 strong) holding a solid defensive position on the north bank of the River Irfon. While he was distracted, an English force launched a surprise attack on an unguarded ford near the smaller river's confluence with the Wye. Outflanked, Llewellyn's army was routed. As he dashed back to salvage what he could, he was killed by an English man-at-arms, Stephen de Frankton. Independent Wales died with him.

Longshanks' conquest took nearly six years and by the time he'd finished had cost the English taxpayers a staggering £173,000 (nearly £35m in today's terms). Of course, purchasing power has changed – as a rule of thumb put the cost of a castle at the equivalent of a modern aircraft carrier. It was a hard-fought series of campaigns. The Welsh inflicted some serious defeats but Edward won in the end. Ruthlessly, he set his seal on the conquest by seeding English towns and colonists then cementing these with an iron ring of mighty castles including Rhuddlan, Harlech, Conwy, Caernarvon and Beaumaris.

The cost of the war, with its consequential drain on the English Exchequer conferred an unexpected boost to parliamentary democracy. The king was forced to rely more heavily on MPs

Reconstruction of Conwy Castle in the early 1300s – on display in the castle. (Hchc2009, Wikimedia Commons, CC BY-SA 3.0)

to provide new tax grants, surely galling for a man of such a pronounced autocratic temperament.

His great fortresses were state-of-the-art 'concentric' castles. They no longer relied upon the final redoubt of a great keep; their strength was spread through strong towers linked by a curtain wall. In fact there were two curtain walls, the outer lower and slighter than the inner (which had towers high enough for archers to shoot across the outer. The style was Byzantine and later Arab, imported back into Europe via the crusades.

Was this great castle-building programme justified or was it just a vast white elephant, an egomaniac's dream? Caernarfon was never fully finished, work on Beaumaris stopped for lack of funds. Yet Conwy and Harlech did withstand sieges and England's grip on Wales was never broken. Happy irony: the tourist revenue they now contribute is a major boost to the Welsh economy.

Having subdued Wales, Edward, from 1296, attempted to add Scotland to his portfolio. Scotland was a tougher nut altogether, bigger, further away and inaccessible. He had no cash left to build another great ring of fortresses, so decided to cannibalise and build up what was already there. Edward, 'Hammer of the Scots', dished out plenty of beatings but never won a decisive victory, never completely extinguished the flame of liberty (though it burned pretty low at times). Finally old age did for him just as he was setting out for another go. It would be hard to say which annoyed him most, mortality or Robert the Bruce.

Marc Morris recounts a remarkable investigation undertaken in the 1950s by A. J. Taylor to identify the true master builder responsible for Longshanks' great concentric ring of Welsh fortresses. He hailed the Savoyard Master James of Saint George (c. 1230–1309) as one of the greatest architects of the Middle Ages. We would go further and describe him as just one of the greatest. Edward, through his father, had a strong connection with the important and strategically placed Duchy of Savoy. It was most likely in 1373, returning from a crusade, that Edward, at St-Georges-d'Esperanche, met Master James. It was Taylor who identified key similarities in unique features seen at Harlech with those found in Savoyard castles.

Master James came to England and is recorded in 1278 as being the master mason for the king's works in Wales. The breadth of his genius at the height of his art are truly breath taking. Building Rhuddlan necessitated canalising the River Clywd (so heavier vessels could navigate up to the castle and provide vital re-supply), a major feat of engineering. By 1285, as chief architect, he was being paid 3s (15p) per day (a skilled mason would normally draw 4d (2p). Harlech, along with Conwy and the incomplete

Faith mattered so the lord needed a private oratory to pursue his devotions. **Chapels** might be located in the keep or great tower (Newcastle) or on a more modest scale in the gatehouse (Prudhoe). In a larger space there was scope for a wider congregation. They exhibit a range of distinctive features such as the Earl of Northumberland's great castle at Warkworth which had a sedile (seat) for the priest and an attached sacristy.

Harlech Castle. (photographed and uploaded by Oosoom, Wikimedia Commons, CC BY-SA 3.0)

Caernarfon and Beaumaris, were his masterpieces. In 1290 he was elevated to Constable of Harlech, a plum appointment.

He followed Edward up to Scotland, though by now likely in his seventies, to undertake upgrades at Linlithgow and Stirling. Even if, as Marc Morris suggests (though we don't necessarily agree), the huge Welsh fortresses were a collective white elephant, the concept, planning and execution of their construction re-defined the nature of castle-building in Britain.

How in such a short time did Master James throw up one of these vast, refined fortresses? Choosing the right site was vital. Edward cunningly constructed his castles with access to coast or river – they could be supplied by water in time of siege. This paid handsome dividends when the king was himself surrounded in Conwy (December 1294–January 1295). Castle building in Wales went hand in hand with town planning. The conquest, to form the basis of lasting new order, had to be economically viable and ideally self-sustaining. Conwy alone cost a staggering £15,000 to build.

Master James would with his royal client seek a good high position, near the coast or a navigable waterway. Solid rock was preferable to shield the finished structure from mining. If a town was also planned then a substantial area would be needed overall. Phase one would see teams of carpenters framing accommodation for tradesmen and soldiers, workshops and a hall for the architect and, very probably, his family. Once marked out the site would be protected by a preliminary perimeter ditch and palisade.

He would already have sketched ideas in his mind. A concentric design perhaps: a series of defended rings, becoming smaller but also stronger towards the core. A castle like Beaumaris, his uncompleted masterpiece, would have a mighty strong inner bailey shielded by a high curtain wall with an outer bailey beyond; also walled but not to the same strength. Both gateways would be flanked by hefty D-shaped towers; those guarding the inner gate would be particularly strong. Both walls would be bolstered by strong cylindrical towers enabling 'enfilade' shooting so enemies couldn't approach the curtain walls unseen.

As well as strong flanking towers, the gates were defended by a series of additional features all intended to make an attacker's life very difficult and, ideally, very short. In a way Master James was pre-empting Clausewitz by six centuries. The castle's defences were designed to wear down an attacker's resolve and resources, blunting his attacks – 'the diminishing power of an offensive', as the German gentleman might have echoed.

Gates, portcullis and drawbridge: Few original gates survive but these were almost invariably timber, ideally oak, double-leaved and side-hung. Typically the gatehouse had two sets, one at each end of the passageway. As an additional deterrent and control, many gatehouses were fitted with a vertically hung timber lattice device called the portcullis which was lowered via winding gear from the level above. The portcullis descended through grooves cut in the masonry. The pointed lower ends of the vertical timbers were usually iron shod to prevent wear. In order to traverse the ditch or moat a retractable wooden bridge, the drawbridge, was added. It was raised or lowered by a further winding mechanism.

The interior design was one of 'enceinte', a courtyard with all the buildings constructed against the inner wall; great hall, kitchens, the king's private quarters (occupied by the steward for most of the time), storehouses, workshops, stables, barracks, smithy, brewery and buttery. The latter was a wine cellar rather than a butter mountain – the name is derived from the French *bouteille*, bottle. Small beer was the standard beverage as water by and large was suspect. Henry II's father died from drinking contaminated water. Longshanks was well aware of the risks.

We can imagine an outer curtain 91 metres long on each of its four sides, 6 metres high and 2.4 metres thick. Towers would have the same bulk but an extra 3 metres in height. The inner curtain would be anything up to 45 metres shorter, but 4.6 metres higher and 1.2 metres thicker. Its towers would soar to 15 metres. This added elevation provided for overlapping shooting from the higher, inner towers. A parapet walk ran around both the outer wall and towers, reached by internal stairs. With the inner wall, access to the parapet was via internal spirals located in the towers. Overall, the idea was for the defender to be able to mass his men at any point of maximum danger. Walls were vertical except at the base where there would be a pronounced splay or 'batter'. This gave additional strength and made an enemy miner's job that bit harder.

While still at the planning and survey stage Master James, backed by the royal writ, would have summoned the English counties to find the labour he needed. In all he'd require perhaps 3,000 craftsmen, tradesmen and labourers and a galaxy of skills: quarry-men, masons, lime mortar-mixers, navvies, carpenters, smiths, metal workers, plumbers, glaziers, joiners and plasterers. Each of these trades would have their own foreman reporting to Master James, who was architect, engineer, quantity surveyor and clerk of works. He was far better paid but he earned every shilling. He was in charge of some of the biggest construction projects in Europe, in modern terms another Thames Barrier or Wembley Stadium.

Smiths would forge many of the hand tools used on site, picks, crowbars, and a variety of saws, spades, shovels, hammers, chisels and axes. The advantage of building on bedrock is that the foundations are already in place. Once the main buildings had been pegged out and levelled construction could begin. By now the place would be a fully fledged building site: a pile of cabins, stores, brew-houses, open kitchens, barrack blocks, sod and canvas for the rank and file, timber with wattle and daub for management. This wasn't just a build, it was a whole industry. It may, for the Welsh patriot, have represented the conqueror's hobnails on his neck but for many it was a source of income, boom times. Vessels would keep watch offshore with a constant sea passage of personnel and materiel.

As quarried stone was shipped/transported to site, teams of hauliers, horses and ox carts would be needed. These in turn might require escorts depending on just how restless the natives actually were. Work on the outer curtain would start first; two skins of ashlar (shaped sandstone blocks), with a core of rubble and mortar. Lime mortar would bind it, the strength of the mix varying depending on use (stronger for bedding and pointing, a weaker slurry for infill).

As the build rose upwards wooden scaffolding would keep pace. Once the wall reached full height, work could begin on the parapet and crenellation. Permanent putlog holes were left at the base of each merlon to facilitate the erection of timber brattices which would provide top cover. Severe winter weather would, by necessity, signal a temporary halt. The on-site staff would be reduced to a skeleton team and the half-completed masonry packed with straw covers to protect newly laid mortar.

With spring, the tempo of activity rose again. More masons would be needed as work on the massive inner curtain with its lofty towers began. With concentric castles, each tower was a separate strength in itself – access from the wall walk could be sealed off if the perimeter was breached. Barred heavy oak doors would create a free-standing bastion.

This represented additional attrition for an enemy. Each tower comprised three stories. The basement was used only for storage – boosting the defenders' capacity to hold out with two upper chambers providing barrack rooms, each heated by its own fire (vented by an internal flue). The roof of each tower was conical in shape, a stout timber frame finished and weatherproofed with stone flags/slates and lead-work. Internal floors were also in timber, corbelled out from the internal walls. Gradually, over a year of continuous work, the familiar shape became visible. The outer and inner curtains would be nearly complete; towers and gatehouses going up.

One tower broke from the standard pattern as it housed the two-storey chapel, fitted with a double-height circular apse, lit by grand tracery windows, finished with ornate (and very expensive) stained glass. The frescoed interior (paintings applied to wet plaster so the pigments would bind fast), would glow with colour and light. Less prosaically, one tower basement room was left as a gaol; access was via a trapdoor in the timber floor above, not much colour or light in there!

Drainage, particularly getting rid of large quantities of human waste, was important. Comfort and ease mattered but so did the basics of sanitation. Medieval disease killed far more people than enemy action. Infection stalked besieger and besieged alike with a fine objectivity. The toilets (garderobes), were set in the thickness of the curtain wall. Illumination was via an extra arrow loop and the stone seat was corbelled out over either a wet gap or the outer ward. These pungent cess pits were cleaned out regularly.

Once the main curtain walls, towers and gatehouses were finished, work could begin on the domestic buildings in the courtyard. Accommodation for the garrison, glad to be free of their cramped, temporary spaces, was probably built first. These were probably half timbered with messing areas on the first floor, stables and storage below. An armoury and armourer's workshop would be built into one end of the main block. Next up was the great hall, a double-storied space maybe 100 feet (30.4 metres) in overall length. Roofed in carved timbers and stone/slate, this grandest of grand spaces was lit by traceried windows and had easy access to the kitchen next door.

The flagged floor would be regularly strewn with fresh aromatic herbs and grasses, the long walls decorated with gorgeous tapestries, the high table placed on a raised dais. Here the king or, by proxy, his steward would entertain people who mattered, visiting dignitaries, garrison knights, influential burghers from the new civilian township (no Welshmen of course). Justice would be dispensed, taxes and rents collected, important council meetings held. The hall combined bling, awe and pragmatism.

If the hall was the stage, the kitchen was backstage. It was a vitally important part of the castle's function, getting it right mattered. At times pressure on the cooks would be immense, producing vast quantities of food for large numbers of guests, probably discerning guests with high expectations. Failing to meet those expectations was not an option. A large space was needed; it would house bread ovens, several fireplaces, storage for foodstuffs and the better end of the wine cellar. Washing and cleaning facilities were a must, so water would be piped directly to the sinks from a large cistern located at the top of an adjacent corner tower. The risk of fire meant it was often some distance from other buildings. Better cold food than hot timbers.

The Black Death

In the 14th century bubonic plague devastated England and, latterly, Scotland. Estimates of what percentage of the population were killed off vary but it was catastrophic, probably at least a third. The further north you went the less severe the contagion. For a while the Scots thought themselves immune – safe from 'the English disease'. They were wrong, a gang of Scottish cattle thieves brought back more than they'd bargained for.

This cataclysm was a game-changer. Acute labour shortages meant those peasants who had previously been tied to the land found themselves in a free or freer market economy. Lords had progressively to rely on wages rather than feudal obligation. If the knight had to bring in swords for hire as part of his garrison strength, relationships changed and he might, for a variety of reasons choose to distance himself to a far greater degree than before. He also wanted more comfort and the idea of privacy was catching on.

Between the Anarchy and Wars of the Roses, England was largely at peace. There was plenty of lawlessness; magnates were forever pursuing their own vendettas. Those flourished under weak kings like Henry VI, when boisterous nobles like Percy and Neville took their grudges onto the streets. Exceptions were the Welsh marches and the northern frontier which was rarely calm. In Bruce's day, after Bannockburn, Scottish light cavalry or hobilars carried fire and sword as far south as Lancashire.

From 1314 till the 'shameful' peace of Northampton 14 years later, Bruce's hobilars, led by able captains like Randolph and Douglas, brutalised and terrorised the North of England. Not until the reign of Edward III did the pendulum of border warfare swing back again. Manors were devastated, lordships ruined. Of course, ruin for some is opportunity for others. The others came by the name of Percy. Hitherto established in Yorkshire they acquired the Barony of Alnwick from slippery Bishop Bek in 1313 and never looked back.

In the 14th century the Percies turned Northumberland and parts of Durham into a mini kingdom. They bought up struggling or bankrupt estates and became the largest landholder in the area. Henry, 4th Baron Percy (confusingly most of them were named Henry), gained an earldom in 1377 from Richard II. That didn't buy too much in the way of loyalty. They backed Bolingbroke in 1399 but soon fell out and rebelled against him four years later.

Rising from a loop in the Coquet, Warkworth Castle, overlooking the village of the same name in Northumberland, is one of England's most evocative castles, its allure enhanced by the mysterious Hermitage grotto just along the river bank. Warkworth is pure picture postcard. The settlement dates certainly from the 8th century, the castle is post conquest.

Late 14th-century tower keep at Warkworth in Northumberland. (Draco2008, Wikimedia Commons, CC BY 2.0)

During the struggle with Scottish kings trying to establish a frontier barrier or Pale in northern England, the place was held by Prince Henry of Scotland but later King Malcolm IV ceded this and other fiefs to Henry II. For a time thereafter it was held by the de Claverings before coming into the 4th baron/1st earl's avaricious grip in 1345.

As an *arriviste* who'd built a personal empire, Henry Percy knew a thing or two about status. He added the very distinctive keep to Warkworth, no grim blank-faced donjon but a suitably grand flourish. John of Gaunt, no friend of Henry's, was building pretty close at Dunstanburgh and the Nevilles, also on the rise, were adding the domestic ranges to Bamburgh. A gentleman needs to compete with his neighbours, especially if he is at odds with both.

If the older Henry was greedy, his son (another Henry but better known as 'Hotspur') was a vainglorious thug whose rebellion ended in blood and tears at Shrewsbury. The old fox dodged the hounds for another five years but the family were in disgrace and bested by their Neville rivals who did very well out of Percy's fall. But if avarice was an overriding Percy trait then so was resilience. Hotspur's son, yet another Henry, clawed back most of his inheritance and the earldom. Most but not all. The Nevilles had picked up some real gems from Percy's broken crown and that led to a series of scuffles in the early 1450s which helped to fan the embers that would burst into flame at St Albans in 1455.

Percy had backed another loser and died on the blood-slicked streets. His son, now the 3rd Earl, went the same way at the battle of Towton (1461). Warwick the Kingmaker's able sibling John, Lord Montagu, netted the vacant earldom and added the tower that bears his name at Warkworth. That 'worm eaten hold of ragged stone' as Shakespeare rather unkindly dismisses the castle. Eventually, Edward IV felt a need to reinstate a Percy and allowed the young 4th Earl into his own. Montagu was compensated but not by anywhere near enough. Disgruntled, he joined in his older brother's conspiracies. Both paid with their lives at Barnet (1471) and the Durham line of the Nevilles was done for. Confusingly, the Westmorland Nevilles had initially backed the other side.

Model of Peveril Castle. (Mike Peel, Wikimedia Commons, CC BY-SA 4.0)

Now the 4th Earl Percy was a far more circumspect character, canny and devious enough to ride with both hare and hounds without falling off. He appeared to work well in partnership with Richard of Gloucester, the new big player in the North with Warwick gone. This entente didn't survive the acid test of Bosworth and Percy moved smoothly into the Tudor sphere. He wasn't going to die a heroic but pointless and expensive death on any battlefield. Nor did he. Rather ingloriously, he fell to a mob protesting about the taxes he was trying to collect; welcome to the English Renaissance.

What he did undertake around 1480 was another burst of building at Warkworth. Even the grand keep wasn't quite modish enough for his aspirations and he re-modelled the bailey, adding a superbly constructed and beautifully detailed hall wing of which the marvellous Lion Tower forms most of what remains.

This was bling on bling, luxury and ostentation, not defence. It's about status through wealth and position as much as peerless knighthood which was steadily being shelved under 'archaic'. It shows that even the extended dynastic and factional brawl between Lancaster and York with all its bloodletting, betrayals and twists hadn't really disturbed the steady move from fortress to mansion. A changing and, despite appearances, more peaceable society was becoming less fissiparous. Besides, there were the guns. Friar Bacon's devilish invention had begun dominating the besieger's art. Traditional castles would need new defences.

Bodiam – fortress or fancy?

Know that of our special grace we have granted and given licence on behalf of ourselves and our heirs, so far as in us lies, to our beloved and faithful Edward Dalyngrigge Knight, that he may strengthen with a wall of stone and lime, and crenellate and may construct and make into a Castle his manor house of Bodyham, [Bodiam] near the sea, in the County of Sussex, for the defence of the adjacent country, and the resistance to our enemies ... In witness of which etc. The King at Westminster 20 October.

Excerpt from the licence to crenellate allowing Edward Dallingridge to build a castle (from the Patent Rolls 1385–89)

Bodiam Castle in East Sussex is one of Britain's most popular castles. It certainly looks the business, wonderfully (or nearly) symmetrical. The walls rise majestically from a wide moat so the structure seems to float on the water. It is beautifully built. While most of the interior is gone, the external structure stands (even if restored by several 19th-century enthusiasts including Lord Curzon). But is it the real deal or, like Scottish Eilean Donan, a carefully wrought fake? Opinions are divided. Sir Edward Dallingridge himself dates from the age of Chaucer and had a slightly Falstaffian air. He probably wasn't a very nice man. Most of his fortune was loot from licensed banditry, the 'Free Companies' who helped themselves during the French Wars. He

Bodiam Castle. (WyrdLight.com, Wikimedia Commons, CC BY-SA 3.0)

served firstly with the Duke of Clarence from 1367 and latterly with the totally disreputable Sir Robert Knolles. He was very good at networking and his connections got him out of hot water on at least one occasion.

As a younger son, he had pretty much to shift for himself, a born opportunist and canny politician. He assiduously built up his position in Sussex. Though he could call himself a gentleman, the family still carried the whiff of trade. He was lucky in a way that during the 1380s the war with France was going badly.

Edward III had kick-started the whole shop of horrors forty years earlier and smitten the French regularly, most notably at Crecy in 1346 and Poitiers a decade after. King David II of Scotland, invading the north in support of his French allies had been roundly thrashed and captured at Neville's Cross. Latterly, the tide had turned. Bertrand du Guesclin, the French king's 'hog in armour' had clawed back much of what had been lost. Edward III and his energetic son the Black Prince were both dead and Richard II wasn't really up to the job. French privateers were terrorising the south coast.

The need to stiffen defences was good for Sir Edward. Bodiam is some distance from the sea but its construction could be justified. Plus, there was bother at home, revolting peasants under Wat Tyler had shaken the social order and Dallingridge, the *nouveau*, was active in suppressing the troubles. In 1383, two years after the rebellion, he was granted a charter allowing weekly markets and an annual fair. With a big invasion scare two years after that, he got his licence to crenellate. Rather than just upgrade his existing manor house he built a new castle. Thanks to the French wars he could afford it.

King Richard probably thought he was getting a proper castle fit to see off any Gallic trespassers. And it probably would have. It is unlikely Bodiam could have withstood a major siege, but it would have been strong enough to withstand any hit-and-run attack by a gang of ruffians looking for easy loot. Sir Edward knew all about ruffianly behaviour.

Bodiam is an enclosure castle, there was never any keep. A range of well-appointed and elegant apartments were grouped around the central courtyard. Sir Edward was a showman, he aimed to dazzle. This wasn't mere ostentation; it was the central plank of his rising status. He was only a few generations away from trade. If it hadn't been for the wars, he would have been nobody, a skint *arriviste*. Marrying well and teaming up with a successful thug like Knolles filled his pockets, and the threat of French invasion gave him his cue. He wasn't one to miss the chance. All the same, there are plenty to question whether Bodiam is a castle or a house dressed up as one?

Look at the wide moat, that's a powerful wet gap obstacle. Access in Sir Edward's day was via a pontoon from the west bank up to a tiny octagonal islet. Once there you had a 90-degree turn towards a barbican before you ever got to the impressive main gatehouse. But there is a flaw. Firstly the lake is 1.8 metres deep and, as the site is elevated and falls away sharply, the waters are held by a mini dam which could easily be broken down.

The walls are high but not very thick, the parapet only 0.3 metres wide – rather puny. Worse, both the southern and eastern walls are pierced low down with large traceried windows. The gatehouses look big and strong, but the wooden gates are very thin and there is no drawbridge. There are gun loops, something of an innovation, but these have a very limited field of fire. We could say that Sir Edward has simply built a sumptuous house and thrown a kind of curtain wall around it. The debate continues but Bodiam, as might be said of later pretentious dwellings, smacks of Queen Anne front and Mary Anne back.

Joyous Garde – Lancelot and Guinevere

Bamburgh must be one of the most photographed of all Britain's great castles. Why not, it sits supreme on its stark outcrop of hard basalt, the last flourish of the Whin Sill that carries Hadrian's Wall before it sinks into the North Sea. It is largely a re-imagining, created by Lutyens to glorify Lord Armstrong: an industrial rather than medieval magnate but one whose wealth still came from the spoils of war. Though by this time that meant supplying other people's rather than fighting his own.

It may well have been an Iron Age fort but certainly formed the kernel of Saxon Ida's new fledgling kingdom. His grandson and successor Flamdwyn gave it to his queen Bebba from whom the place gets its name. Happily for the Northumbrians, St Aidan, from his cell on the Farnes, was able to summon God's assistance for a timely shift in wind direction when fearsome Penda of Mercia attempted to burn down the palisade. Bamburgh was the capital of the growing kingdom and housed such important relics as the head and hand of St Oswald.

Inevitably the place got trashed by the Vikings and the core of what we see today is Norman. Before then, before even Ida, it might have been called in Old English *Dinguardi*. Those attuned to Arthurian romance might work out that Malory anglicised or rather Frenchified this to 'Joyous Garde'. We're way beyond history here and firmly into myth but we do know numerous Iron Age forts had a second lease of life after the end of the Roman occupation.

It was entrusted to the First Knight Lancelot who, as we know, was in love with Guinevere. Evil Mordred and his mate Agravain kept a close watch on the pair, grassing them up to a saddened King Arthur who allowed Mordred with a dozen men at arms to bring them both in. Honest Bors warns Lancelot who, though he doesn't wear his mail, keeps his sword hidden in the folds of his cloak when he goes to pay an evening call on the queen.

Mordred turns up mob handed but Lance is ready and does for Agravain and all of the rest except Mordred who takes to his heels. Lancelot flees Camelot but leaves the queen, sure the king will show mercy. He doesn't. Guinevere is condemned to the stake with Mordred as impresario. The generally unlamented Agravain was Gawain's brother who now, understandably turns against Lancelot. Everyone thinks Lancelot will try to rescue Guinevere. He does and Mordred bottles it again. Another two of Gawain's brothers are cut down in the melee. Gawain is now really very irritated and spearheads Arthur's retaliatory strike against Joyous Garde where Lancelot and Guinevere are holding out.

It's a full-blown siege, a mini civil war, just what creepy Mordred is hoping for. Gawain is a man possessed by revenge and the many fights before the walls are hard and costly for both sides. Arthur himself is in serious trouble at one stage but Lancelot, the really good guy, saves him. This is the sign for a truce and then cease fire. Guinevere is sent back to her husband, though not as a sacrifice and Lancelot accepts exile back in his native Brittany. It's not history as we know it but it is a cracking story which has kept poets, novelists and filmmakers in business ever since.

CHAPTER 3

BORDER BASTION – HARBOTTLE CASTLE

1296–1603

Redesdale and Tynedale … the only two allegiances of the warriors of these wild regions was loyalty towards their own clans.

G. M. Trevelyan

Harbottle is a perfect case study for a border bastion. Aside from its long and violent history, it, and the wild lands it sits in, are largely unchanged. It's much ruined; generations of enterprising locals with no regard for heritage used the former stronghold for building supplies. The entire village is built from pilfered stones, major recycling. One thing we can say for Harbottle – it's no Bodiam, it's very much the real thing.

If you stand at the Drake Stone – an uncompromising, great square boulder 9 metres high and weighing in at over 1,800 tonnes left behind by the titanic grind of some prehistoric glacier – you can look down on the linear settlement below. Behind you runs Harbottle Crag with the long spine of Gallows Edge – fittingly the ideal spot for hangings.

The Coquet winds lazily around the northern flank of the castle plateau toward that sharp bend known as the Devil's Elbow. Across the river, Camp Hills are said to be where invading armies pitched their bothies and banners. Nearby Park House denotes the site of the lord's deer park. It all looks wonderfully calm, yet you can frequently hear the roar of the guns behind you from the MoD ranges.

The fortress itself sits on a steep-sided, boat-shaped ridge running east to west with the Coquet flowing around almost three sides. On the fourth or south flank, the village sits in a shallow groove that marks a former line of the waters. Strategically, this place is a cork in a bottle. To the north, ground dips quite sharply towards the river and terraces have been formed from historic land spill. There's a natural spring which rises from just below the barmkin (a form of outer courtyard) , with evidence of attempts at water management. The bailey ditch which encroaches from the west has been partially filled by a more modern track. Whether the slippage is pre or post construction is impossible to say. Four stone clearance heaps stand on the largest of these terrace features but there is no obvious traces of cultivation.

Judging by the name of the place (which is early old English) the value of this eminently defensible location predates the Norman Conquest. The position is ideal with good all-round vision, that 'long view' so valued on the border. Scouts on the higher Lord's Seat to the west could give warning of any impending attack

Hoardings, machicolations and murder holes:
A hoarding is an enclosed, timber framed fighting gallery cantilevered out over the battlements. It gives the defender's troops considerable additional cover and a killing view down towards the vulnerable base of the wall. Projecting timbers are themselves a risk so these were replaced in stone, creating an aperture through which arrows and all manner of unpleasant things could shower down on impudent attackers close to the walls. The wonderfully named murder-hole refers to a particular type of machicolation normally seen on gatehouses (though these may have been intended as much for ease of re-supply).

Murder holes in the gatehouse of Bodiam Castle. (Canadacow, Wikimedia Commons, CC BY 3.0)

and the site dominates the line of Clennel Street, winding over Bloodybush Edge and Windy Gyle (well named) to the border, one of the principal routes across the marches. Just south at Holystone, the old Roman route, the 'swire' from Low Learchild to High Rochester, crosses the valley. The spur on which the castle sits divides the lower and upper reaches of Coquetdale. The higher ground west, hemmed in by steep-sided hills was open pasture.

Harbottle Castle and its history are inextricably linked to the powerful Umfravilles, Lords of Redesdale, marcher barons and frontiersmen. We tend to assume that the borderland was, from the outset, an embattled and much fortified landscape. This isn't necessarily so. It is more likely that the tempo of conflict stepped up after the onset of the Three Hundred Years War between England and Scotland (more on that later); the steady up-grading of defences at manorial castles such as Aydon near Corbridge would certainly suggest this:

William by the Grace of God king of England and duke of Normandy, to all his men whether French and English or Norman, greeting: Know you that I have given to my kinsman Robert de Umfravill, knight, lord of Tours in Vian, otherwise called Robert with the Beard ['cum barba'], the lordship, valley and forest with all castles, manors, with lands, woods, pastures, pools with all appurtenances and royal franchises, formerly Mildred son of Akmans, late lord of Redesdale and which came into our hands by conquest To have and hold to the said Robert and his heirs, of my and my heirs, kings of England, by the service of defending the same against enemies and wolves forever with that sword which I had by my side when I entered Northumbria etc....

This is rousing stuff, almost Tolkienesque and, like Tolkien, is probably just as much fiction. The deed was unearthed in 1641 by the antiquary Dodsworth, in Latin of course and dated 10 July 1076. Most subsequent writers cast doubt on its authenticity and there's no agreement as to the actual origins of the Umfravilles. It seems unlikely that Robert-with-the-Beard would have been old enough to have charged at Senlac Hill, though Hodgson overcomes the timeline question by offering the notion there was an earlier Robert and that, as Northumberland County History argues, this particular Robert could have crossed the channel in 1066.

Even if the charter is a fake, it is probably a very old fake, created to justify the holding of the Lordship by subsequent generations though we can be sure the Umfraville connection is an ancient one. In terms of the historical record we can date a Robert de Umfraville from an entry in the Pipe Roll for 1130/31. This Robert seems to have been in the following/affinity of the anglophile David I of Scotland who spent a very long apprenticeship at the English court and was created Earl of both Huntingdon and Northampton.

Robert's son Odinel I succeeded his father and his career is well attested. He appears as a witness to a range of Scottish charters between 1144 and 1153. Before 1158, he also witnessed Henry II of England's grant of the churches of Newcastle and Newburn to the canons of St Mary of Carlisle. From then on we can trace the line through the whole turbulent era to its final extinction and the story of Harbottle Castle is, in many ways, a saga of the Umfravilles.

Odinel I was succeeded by his son Odinel II. The Umfravilles first strongholds were at Prudhoe and the impressive motte at Elsdon before building at Harbottle began around 1157. This site is far better suited to the defence of Redesdale – the location described by Richard de Umfraville in the following century as 'usefully planted on the marches of Scotland towards the Great Waste [those wilder reaches of the upland border dales]'.

Following his conquest, the Conqueror needed strong warlords planted on his several borders. The line of the Tweed had been fixed after the Battle of Carham in 1018 but, in the next generations after Hastings, kings of Scotland had their eye on an extended frontier or 'Pale' which would stretch as far south as the Tees. David I, for all his anglophile sentiments, tried to take this ground with the sword. He didn't do too well and the northern barons smashed his army at Northallerton in 1138, fighting beneath the fabulous banner of St. Cuthbert, their talisman; an event known as the Battle of the Standard. Tolkien would have loved it.

Northern estates or fiefs were not regarded as plums, richer, more settled pastures in the south went to those greater lords who'd stood beneath Duke William's flag at Hastings. Nonetheless, the military class of Liberty afforded sufficient privilege and quasi-autonomy to attract those wilder spirits into the even wilder frontier-land, the 'threap' between two nations whose ongoing history was not destined to be one of friendship. Their job was to consolidate and hold, not just against the Scots; they were expected to curb the worst excesses of their robust marcher subjects, pretty much a full-time job in itself.

If indeed Robert-with-the-Beard got his lordship directly from the Conqueror or if the award came later, the grant was for the valley and forest of Redesdale in 'comitatu' – a shire to be held in private hands. Despite a brief alarum in the reign of John, the Umfravilles would hang on until 1436, nearly four centuries. In feudal terms Redesdale was a barony or chief manor of Harbottle which by 1290 included the manors of: Otterburn, Monkridge, Elsdon, Garretshields, Woodburn, The Leams, Troughend,

Chesterhope, Lynshiels, Bromhope and Corsenside. A lord needs a castle. On the border this would always be doubly necessary.

In plan, the original castle is similar to others in Northumberland at Mitford, Alnwick and Norham with a strong motte standing in the middle of the south flank with the kidney shaped bailey circling on three sides. In a later phase of building, the bailey was bisected north/south by a stone outer wall, creating an inner and outer space. This second phase (in stone) likely dates from the early 13th century. The castle William the Lion trashed was probably still timber but the stronger reconstruction withstood a siege in 1296, though it fell again to Bruce in 1318. Sir Nicklaus Pevsner describes the site as 'one of the finest medieval earthworks in the county'.

After 1154, Henry II was attempting to deal with Scottish claims to parts of northern England. He made a deal with Malcolm IV whereby the Scottish king would abandon any pretensions to control the Carlisle area and Northumberland in return for being made Earl of Huntingdon. As the Scots had failed militarily to enforce their territorial aspirations, this clearly had an appeal. At the same time, Henry strengthened the border

The Shell Keep: It may have been a feature of motte and bailey that the tower on its motte was enclosed by a timber palisade, a smaller version of that circling the bailey and that there were additional buildings besides the strong tower. This idea is then, literally set in stone, with the later introduction of the shell or hollow circular keep. These are a feature of mainly the late 11th and 12th centuries – though Harbottle Castle has a shell keep which endures into the Tudor era.

just in case anyone changed their minds. The Tweed had been the official line since Carham over two centuries before and now became the (largely) fixed frontier. Berwick would change hands fourteen times in the course of the border wars. Redesdale was the front line and would remain so until 1603.

Strong keeps at Newcastle, Bamburgh and Wark on Tweed were rebuilt or strengthened. Bishop le Puisset, whose see of Durham controlled Norham 'the queen of border fortresses', was persuaded to give the place a substantive makeover. In 1157 Henry gave Odinel de Umfraville instructions to shift his key stronghold from Elsdon to Harbottle. He was to rebuild in stone (though more likely, in the first instance, he stuck to timber). Stone was clearly a better option. A timber stockade, aside from being vulnerable to fire, had a working life of only thirty years, stone endured. One difficulty, such as the Umfravilles discovered at Prudhoe, was that man-made motte and bailey, while compact enough to take the weight of timber, might not stand the far greater bulk of stone.

It was also in 1157 that Scots King, William the Lion, received the Liberty of Tynedale as a further quid pro quo for giving up his wider designs on Northumberland. That didn't deter the Scottish king from poking around in English affairs in 1172 and, two years later, coming down again in full force. William laid siege to Prudhoe Castle, the Umfraville redoubt but was seen off. He fell back to have a crack at Alnwick, though not before he'd taken and slighted Harbottle. One wing of his army duffed up Warkworth and immolated the terrified inhabitants inside their own church. These border wars weren't nice; the veneer of chivalry masked a stark reality of terror and atrocity. Both sides had a great deal of practice.

The king should have remembered what happened to Shakespeare's Malcolm at Alnwick, an unfortunate precedent. A relief force of English knights, including Odinel de Umfraville, beat up his quarters in a dawn raid and caught him in the rout.

So the Lion's abortive campaign ended in a costly debacle with him in irons. The king of Scots was obliged to bend his knee and do homage for his lands to Henry II, though the Liberty of Tynedale was restored to him the following year and would be held by his successors for a century and a half. Richard the 3rd Lord of Redesdale also did good service in the Crusades and became Richard the Lionheart's Captain of Acre.

Although the Scots were beaten, they'd left a trail of destruction behind. Odinel II was awarded a grant of £20.00 from the rental of the mines at Carlisle to pay his garrison at Prudhoe. After William the Lion's capture, Odinel also received a share of the recovered plunder, a lifetime grant of the manor of Elton in Yorkshire and netted the forfeited estates of Thomas de Muschamp, Baron of Wooler.

Odinel made numerous grants to religious houses though he was very much at odds with the prior of Tynemouth. He died leaving substantial debts and was succeeded by his son Robert. It was only after Robert's own death in 1195 that his successor, a younger brother Richard, paid off the last of the cash owing to Jewish financiers from York. At about this time, the citizens of York devised their own very nasty final solution to local debt crises by murdering the entire Jewish community.

Richard de Umfraville (the first) fell foul of King John and was obliged to surrender all of his four sons as hostages plus Prudhoe Castle as surety for his good behaviour. This didn't stop him 'coming out' with rebellious barons in 1215 and his estates were duly confiscated. This fall from grace endured for five years till he was fully reinstated. On his death in 1226, his eldest son Gilbert succeeded as Lord of Redesdale and Baron of Prudhoe.

Gilbert was a leading magnate in the north and served Henry III on a spread of important missions. His second wife Matilda was the daughter and heiress of Malcolm, Earl of Angus, and widow of John Comin. As well as fresh lands, the Umfravilles gained a claim to the Scottish earldom of Angus. Gilbert's son, another of the same name, had a distinguished career in Longshanks' service campaigning in Wales, Gascony and Scotland. Gilbert was what might be described as a rough diamond. These marcher lords were no 'plaster saints'. Hardened by near continuous military service and presumably enjoying themselves, they weren't over burdened by awe of superior authority, not even so terrifying a figure as Longshanks.

Though we may doubt the authenticity of the supposed original grant from William I, Gilbert, as 5th lord, relied on its terms to see off an attempt by the crown to usurp or take back his judicial rights attaching to the Liberty. Despite his loyal service to the crown, he was ordered by Edward I to hand over certain alleged 'malefactors' but demurred on the grounds that his own justices were empowered to hear such cases in Harbottle. Gilbert, refusing to be bullied by Longshanks (who knew a thing or two about bullying), reminded his sovereign that he was the one who could make judicial appointments within his fiefdom. He remained solely entitled to any profits from litigation, could seize the goods of criminals and generally beat up their holdings.

The legal argument was that the Liberty was granted in grand 'sergeant' – 'by the exercise of defending that part of the county forever from enemies and wolves, with that sword which King William had by his side when he entered Northumberland' – an echo of the ancient claim. 'Wolves' meant not only four-legged predators but human outlaws, 'Wolf's heads'. As it happens, the last of the canine variety to be hunted down in England is said to have been killed at Harbottle. Gilbert's unrepentant defiance brought him into conflict with Longshanks' authoritarian temperament and the king, much as he valued his subject's sword-arm, would never pass on an opportunity to clip his wings.

Not entirely surprising, Gilbert was a law unto himself in his own domain. In July 1267 he sent a company of distinctly shady characters to forcibly eject William Douglas from the manor of Rawdon near Girsonfield. These ruffians applied themselves to their task with considerable energy, pilfering and abusing at will. The unlucky Douglas and one of his sons were thrown into the cells at Harbottle before Umfraville accused William of treason, though he himself was later accused of murdering his captive's son.

Gilbert was an enthusiastic practitioner of the borderer's art of extracting 'black rent' or blackmail, blatant thuggery. Even his relative William, who held Elsdon, wasn't immune. When this importunate kinsman dared hold a market thinking he had acquired such commercial rights by view of his tenancy, Gilbert sent his heavies in to trash the stalls!

For a suitable wife (one who brought a decent dowry), Gilbert chose Elizabeth, daughter of Alexander de Comyn, Earl of Buchan, further cementing the family's links to Scottish aristocracy. He died in 1307 and was buried inside his own chapel in Hexham Priory church in a suitably splendid tomb (part of which survives).

He was succeeded by his second, surviving son Robert who also became Earl of Angus. Robert, like his father had a distinguished career, though interrupted by a spell in a Scottish gaol after his capture at Bannockburn. He was soon ransomed and active again until his own death in 1325, being buried before the high altar in Newminster abbey near Morpeth. Through his first wife Lucy he'd inherited substantial estates in both Yorkshire and Lincolnshire. His second wife Alienore was from the powerful family of the Earls of Clare.

Loos and lavers: Basic human functions don't alter – any castle with a booming population needs facilities. In a castle you had to be careful, disease was potentially a greater killer than any mortal foe. These had to be cleaned out so were normally fitted into externally projecting towers supported on stone corbels. This meant waste fell outside the walls often into the moat. Now this exposed chute was a tactical weakness often guarded by a suspended stone to prevent any ungentlemanly attacking archer shooting upwards at a most exposed moment. Washing too was important; niche-mounted sinks with drain pugs called lavers (from the French *laver* to wash), were installed as were substantial sinks and drainage facilities in food preparation areas.

Castle toilets at La Bâtiaz. (AJ Marshall, Wikimedia Commons, CC BY-SA 4.0)

Harbottle Castle passed through numerous transitions during its long career – nearly half a millennium all told. Initially, a causeway crossed the bailey ditch, coming in from the east and at the base of the motte which wasn't directly accessible. It could only be approached from the west, from within the bailey. The stone castle, shell keep, cross wall and middle gate (completed around 1200), comprise phase one. The masonry curtain wall which bisects the original, larger outer bailey was finished with the addition of a strong tower in the north-east corner.

The shell keep, complete with projecting towers, was constructed on the top of the motte. A century later phases two and three saw the gateway being rebuilt on a much grander scale. This was in time for Bruce, after 1318, to demand the castle be trashed and there are traces of damage inflicted at that time. The outer bailey was probably abandoned about then and the defensive enclosure marked by the cross wall which now became the outer perimeter, with the rebuilt middle gate serving as a main entrance.

Castles changed immeasurably in the course of the medieval era. This wasn't just the transition from timber to stone or from great tower to concentric style. In the earlier period it was all about communal living, the lord lived alongside his family and retainers. Gradually, this shifted as gentlemen sought more private family accommodation, distancing themselves from sweaty commoners. Standards of luxury and refinement rose: providing a running water supply for the lord was not uncommon. He retained the great defensive donjon as a refuge but took his ease in more comfortable domestic buildings ranged round the inner bailey.

Within the shell keep at Harbottle, the Umfraville Lord would have had his hall, kitchen and private chapel. His followers would have been accommodated in the bailey below. Most of what we see on the motte is Tudor rebuilding, so the original layout is harder to fathom. What we do need to understand is that the structure was not purely defensive. All-round defence would be a priority but the place represents the very badge of Umfraville authority. It would have soared loftily above the humble cabins of the ordinary folk clustered around and below, a symbol of feudal power, not just the lord's writ but, through him, that of the crown of England. It was intended to impress as well as intimidate.

Many medieval castles in England, the majority even, were never attacked. By the fifteenth century gentlemen were thinking far more of comfort than war, their strongholds morphing into country houses. Even the long cataclysm of the Wars of the Roses didn't produce many sieges, really only those of Harlech and Bamburgh (see chapter 5). On the marches it would always be different. Harbottle was still a functioning castle well into the Tudor age. Even after the development of artillery had rendered medieval constructions redundant, the terrain and non-existent roads made transporting great guns a near impossibility.

Despite the harshness of the northern frontier, great lords such as the Umfravilles would have retained a full household. Their sheriff or keeper was a person of note who could deputise for the lord in his absence. The Umfravilles would have employed stewards of the various household offices, cooks, clerks, personal servants, almoners, vintners, bakers, brewers, smiths and farriers, armourers, bowyers, fletchers, a personal chaplain, barber-surgeons, tutors, carpenters, joiners, masons, roofers, personal servants and ladies' maids.

This wasn't the world of *Downton Abbey* or *Upstairs, Downstairs.* No green baize doors; the lord would be on first-name terms with his people yet be served on bended knee. His authority was so absolute it didn't require underlining. He wasn't some nouveau riche. Social mobility was almost unheard of. His superior, Olympian status was part of the unchallenged natural order. There was no concept of equality, the feudal pyramid was generally fixed and he was from the very top tier or near enough.

Harbottle was a living, heaving entity, an entire, self-contained community. Looking at the empty fragments, it's hard to envisage just what it was like in the 13th century, newly finished in stone. It would have been crammed. Men, women and children would have been crowded into the bailey, barrack rooms, kitchens, smithies, brew-house, privies, store rooms and stables. Odours would have been pungent and mixed. Nobody would have been idle.

Everything had to be humped by hand, keeping the walls in readiness required constant maintenance, some part or parts

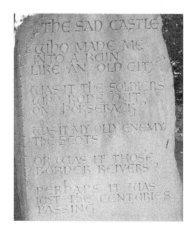

Sad Castle – Child's Poem at Harbottle Castle. (Author's own)

would have been under near constant construction. Sheep, cattle, goats and horses, from the lord's mighty (and mighty expensive) destrier to the more humble garrons of his affinity would be competing for space. The ring of armourer's and smith's hammers would be constantly sounding through the overcrowded air.

In time of calm or relative calm, the place was like a walled and fortified mini-township. In times of war (which were quite often), it would have bristled. Timber hoardings would have appeared above the battlements, creating fighting platforms for archers. Ditches would have been deepened and possibly planted with obstacles and an additional gateway defence, a barrier or wooden extension to the barbican might have been thrown up. That flaming Umfraville banner would fly defiantly above the keep. There would have been readiness. That need never went away.

At any one time the fighting garrison would have numbered no more than say a couple of knights, a dozen men at arms and perhaps a score of archers. This would be regularly swollen by local marchers, an ad hoc militia, boisterous and unruly, *boreales bobinantes* ['roaring northerners'] as their more settled southern contemporaries called them; rough, ready and rapacious, a private army and none too precious.

Horrified southerners recoiled at the barbarity of these thuggish marchers when they swept south under Margaret of Anjou's Lancastrian flag in 1461. The chronicles speak of an orgy of grand larceny, an odyssey of thieving, accompanied by savagery, intimidation and much worse. That is of course a southern view and it may not have been quite that bad but it was clearly quite bad enough.

Once the castle had contracted behind its straight east wall, the area beyond may have been abandoned. There is evidence of ridge and furrow ploughing over what had been the outer bailey. The overall condition had deteriorated again by the middle of the 14th century, constantly buffeted by Scottish raids. Then, during period four, the place got another makeover with work on a drawbridge and barbican. By 1438, when Harbottle is held by the Talbot (Tailbois) family, the keep was in fit condition to house the constable and his household.

Maintaining local forces needed a sound revenue stream; the crown was at best parsimonious. Otterburn was likely the most valuable single holding within the lordship, rated at 2½ knights' fees and like Harbottle Castle itself, retained by the Umfraville Lord rather than tenanted. Gilbert de Umfraville attempted to deprive Longshanks of the 40 marks (13s 4d or say 65p), due from his estate to the crown as death duties and ward-ship fees by granting a late tenancy to one of his affinity. Tax avoidance is not a modern phenomenon.

By the mid-13th century a third of the tenancies were held on military tenure while others were parcelled out as 'petty serjeanty' – rent being met by a gift in kind made annually to the lord. Carucates at Elsdon and Otterburn, together with a 12-acre parcel in Ravenshope, each went for a pound of pepper. An additional tenement in Greensomehillslea provided a pound of cumin.

The Umfravilles held Prudhoe, Ovingham, Elsdon and Bothal but Harbottle seems to have been their principal seat. Despite the ravaging of 1174, the Liberty was probably relatively settled in the 13th century. If there had been frequent alarums it is unlikely Richard de Umfraville would have found himself in court over his failure to acquire a licence to crenellate, which led to an order to dismantle unlicensed fortifications.

This was in fact the consequence of an action begun by Philip of Ulcotes, a former sheriff of Northumberland whose own hold was at Nafferton. He'd tried to build without a licence. This always raised royal hackles harking back to the anarchy of Stephen and Matilda's wars when feuding magnates threw up fresh castles at will. Whether Ulcotes was prompted by spite or rivalry we can't say. Richard was censured in the first instance but on appeal was in turn successful; arguing the strengthening of his works had been 'with the consent and by the order of King Henry II'.

Various border surveys were carried out when English kings were leading their armies over the Channel to bash the French.

That of 1415, undertaken prior to the Agincourt campaign, lists Sir Robert as owner. Though in fact Sir Gilbert, his nephew, currently serving in France, was the actual lord. Later reports, from the 16th century, provide much useful detail:

> On the south side stood the keep, on a conical hill, rising steeply out of the hill on which the other parts of the castle were placed ... Of small extent is the area on the top, so that the erections there, though high were never of great extent... The hall of which the foundations remain, was 48 feet long and 30 feet broad. The two baileys are overlooked by the keep, the inner one lying towards the north west, and the outer one to the north-east, and they are still divided from each other by a wall, partially ruined, running from the keep to the outer curtain wall...
>
> Here too were the draw well, the kitchen, the brew-house, the bake-house, and the horse-mill... Fragments there are of a tower on the north side where, probably, the postern was situated, which required an iron gate, six feet 9 inches high, and 3 feet 9 inches broad. On the east side stood the barbican, or entrance gateway, whose iron gates were 10 feet 3 inches high and 9 feet 9 inches broad. A projecting tower was incorporated in the wall north of the gate. The outer wall was 6 feet thick and 27 feet high. Within the outer bailey were the stables, with lofts above them which were used as granaries and lodgings for the garrison.

What had distinguished Harbottle during the medieval era was that it represented a great baronial castle. In the 16th century this changed – moving from magnatial fortress to crown bastion. The Tailbois were not the Umfravilles. After the Wars of the Roses, they had little interest in their northern outpost, preferring easier estates in flatter Lincolnshire. This is not the end of the castle story though, the place features throughout the 16th century as a key link in the chain of border defences and as a deterrent, partially anyway, to 'the thieves of Redesdale'.

During the violent and troubled era of the Tudor march-lands in the 16th century, Harbottle got a number of makeovers though the picture, as reported in numerous contemporary surveys, was often one of neglect and decay. Tudor princes wanted strong defences; they just didn't like paying for them. In the run up to Flodden, it served as the base for Thomas 'Bull' Dacre, middle march warden, whose feared red bull banner floated over more than a few scraps. The Bull was something of a bulldog, steeped in the treacherous quicksand of cross-border affairs, one who knew James IV quite well. Indeed, he would be the one who identified the mangled, stiffening corpse dragged from the pile on the morning after Flodden.

An early Tudor innovation was the addition of gun loops punched through the walls of the shell-keep – two of these survive today. What is unusual about Harbottle is that this type is normally only seen north of the border where early-16th-century castle-owners were studding their towers and barmkins with a fashionable rash of gun-ports. Harbottle's date from around 1509 and there is a Scottish blockhouse at Dunbar from this period which exhibits similar features. Quite why gun ports suddenly proliferated more in Scotland isn't easy to say. It may have been a matter of prestige, or reflect lower levels of state control. It wasn't because the Scottish gentry were more quarrelsome; feuds flourished with equal venom on both sides of the line.

It seems probable that the loops were intended for early hand-held firearms. Possibly these were breech-loaders – 'cutthoatis' or 'heidsteikis', muzzle loading hackbutts or arquebuses. This term comes from the German 'hackenbusche' which the French prettified into 'harquebus'. The English just dropped the 'h'. These were not sophisticated pieces of kit. The early guns, sometimes cast in bronze were fired by means of a hot wire or lighted match poked through the touch-hole.

There was no standardisation of calibres – they varied between 12 mm to 36 mm. The crude wooden stock did not do much either for aiming or for absorbing the massive recoil. In the fifteenth century these 'gonnes' could be fitted with an iron lug below the barrel which enabled the shooter to loop the weapon over stone or timber defences. This would have helped a little.

Firing an arquebus. (Viollet-le-Duc, Wikimedia Commons)

Norham Castle from the South East. (Pasicles [CC0], Wikimedia Commons)

But by then Harbottle was strictly a castle: the owner did not live there. It was more of a fort now, a state-run outpost on a tricky frontier. When that finally disappeared after James VI of Scotland became James I of England, the place sank into history and the new Harbottle Castle was a comfortable country house. It looks nothing like the original, though the ruins provided the building materials.

Marmion

Sir William Marmion was a Lincolnshire knight. One day, at a banquet in his native shire, he was presented with a fine helmet, given to him by a lady admirer. However, there was a catch. In order to 'earn' his handsome headgear the knight had to ride out and do great deeds of chivalric valour ...

Norham Castle stands on the south bank of the Tweed west of Berwick, a great, square Norman tower with two wards or baileys. It was one of England's strongest border bastions. It was also 'the most dangerous place in England' because it was besieged by the annoyingly persistent Scots. There was nothing for it but to pack his bags and his sword and ride north.

Knights on both sides would enliven the tedium of siege warfare by tourneying with each other. This jousting was as much a preparation for war as sport. Knights would ride at each other with levelled lances trying to knock an opponent off his horse. The winner took the loser's horse and armour – an expensive loss.

Philip de Mowbray, the Scots governor of Berwick had arrived with a troop of picked borderers to stiffen the besiegers. These newcomers were fresh and aggressive, ready to keep up a barrage of taunts towards the weary defenders. Grey had a cunning plan. Marmion would ride out alone and take the entire Scottish force on singlehanded! While, the enemy was distracted, the garrison would launch a surprise attack.

So Sir William Marmion rode out through the gate named after him. This was the very stuff of legend: a lone paladin takes on large numbers of angry Scotsmen. Hooves rattled, then thundered on the turf as Scottish cavalry swept down on the solitary Englishman. Marmion was engulfed, his precious helmet taking many a knock as he hacked and slashed wildly in the melee, taking off an arm here, a leg there, arterial blood spurting in bright, satisfying arcs.

As the jubilant attackers closed in for the kill, the gates of the fortress swung open and a steel-tipped avalanche of English riders erupted. The Scots came to an astonished halt, their ranks broke and their whole besieging force dissolved into an ignominious rout. Both Sir William Marmion and Norham were safe! Was the lady happy with this valour we have to wonder?

CHAPTER 4

THE DEVIL'S INVENTION

1487–1513

Artillerymen believe the world consist of two types of people; other Artillerymen and targets.

Anonymous

Ultima ratio regum (the final argument of kings)

Inscription on French cannons, on order of Louis XIV

THE SUN KING WAS NOT WRONG. Cannon first make their appearance on the field of Crecy in 1346. Bell shaped monsters shooting large darts, they were pretty crude and rather ineffective. Nonetheless, this was definitely the shape of things to come. By the time Henry V came to besiege Harfleur in 1415, he brought a full train of artillery – not a trebuchet in sight. The nature of warfare had shifted. Guns were *the* game-changer and would now dominate siege warfare. The long brawl between Lancaster and York, saw rivers of blood flowing but not that many sieges. Not until the axis of fighting had shifted to Northumberland, after the wake of Towton in 1461, and sputtered on for three more years. King Henry maintained his Lilliputian court at Bamburgh, as ever a spectator of his own story.

After the bare flush of a fight at Hexham in May 1464, the House of Lancaster's tenuous foothold in the north was

Alnwick Castle. (Phil Thomas, Wikimedia Commons, CC BY 2.0)

eliminated along with most of their leadership. Barely two weeks later John Neville, Lord Montagu, knelt before King Edward IV and his court at York and in the presence of both of his brothers, was elevated to the Earldom of Northumberland. Whilst at his northern capital Edward ratified a peace treaty with the Scots, securing a truce for fifteen years. Richard Neville Earl of Warwick (the infamous 'Kingmaker'), as the king's lieutenant was charged with the recovery of the three key border fortresses, Bamburgh, Alnwick and Dunstanburgh, still held by the scraps of old King Henry's defeated forces.

To assist in these operations, Edward had assembled a formidable siege train, 'the great ordnance of England', the bombards "Edward', 'Dijon', 'London', 'Newcastle' and 'Richard Bombartel'. The sight of these great guns was sufficient to overawe the shaken defenders at Alnwick, which capitulated on 23 June, followed, the following day, by Dunstanburgh.

Though perhaps the greatest of the Northumbrian fortresses Bamburgh was not built to withstand cannon and the deployment of the royal train before the massive walls gave notice. The Earl of Warwick dispatched his own and the king's herald, Chester, to formally demand the garrison's surrender. Quarter was offered to the commons but both Sir Ralph Grey and another of the Nevilles (from the Westmoreland lot who'd backed the wrong horse), were excluded from any terms. As' out of the King's grace without any redemption.' Grey, with nothing to lose, stayed defiant. He had 'clearly determined within himself to live or die in the castle.' The heralds gave fair warning:

> The King, our most dread sovereign lord, specially desires to have this jewel whole and unbroken by artillery, particularly because it stands so close to his ancient enemies the Scots, and if you are the cause that great guns have to be fired against its walls, then it will cost you your head, and for every shot that has to be fired another head, down to the humblest person within the place.

So began the only siege bombardment of the Wars of the Roses. The big guns 'Newcastle' and 'London' were positioned, sighted, loaded and began firing, crashing like the crack of doom with a great sulphurous cloud of filthy smoke drifting over the walls. Whole sections of masonry were blasted by round-shot and crashed into the sea. A lighter gun, 'Dijon', fired into the chamber wherein Sir Ralph Grey had established his HQ in the eastern gatehouse; he was injured and rendered insensible when one of these rounds brought down part of the roof.

Humphrey Neville, ever the survivor, seized the moment of his ally's fall to seek terms, securing clemency for the garrison and, cleverly, for himself. The dazed Sir Ralph was tied to his horse and dragged as far as Doncaster to be tried by Sir John Tiptoft, Earl of Worcester and Constable of England. One of the indictments lodged against him was that he 'had withstood and made fences against the king's majesty, and his lieutenant, the worthy lord of Warwick, as appeareth by the strokes of the great guns in the king's walls of his castle of Bamburgh.' Grey was executed on 10 July – the war in the north was, at last, over. But the guns weren't finished.

It was on a wet, blustery afternoon in late summer that King James IV of Scotland committed his army to battle against an

Castles were centres of justice and administration so they needed a **prison** wing. Standards of accommodation varied according to status. The well-heeled could buy more comfortable quarters; the penniless were often dropped via a trap door into a basement vault of unspeakable squalor. A legend attaches (one of many) to Hermitage Castle. The Douglas laird dumped some unfortunate rival into his own dungeon then went off on crusade and forgot all about the poor fellow who starved to death. Hexham Gaol built in the 14th century is the first purpose-built gaol and the pit for common thieves isn't somewhere you'd want to be.

English force led by Thomas Howard, Earl of Surrey. Only the monument atop Piper's Hill by the pleasant if unremarkable north Northumbrian village of Branxton marks the site of the battle which followed, so small a village that *Remembering Flodden* are constructing a visitor centre in a disued phone box, the smallest information point in Britain!

By the early years of the 16th century artillery had become the dominant arm in siege warfare and indeed had been so for nearly a century. These monsters were fired from ground level and from behind a hinged, timber shutter rather like a very much larger version of the archer's mantlet. This provided some cover for the gunner, his mate and matrosses. Most guns loaded at the breech, having a removable block shaped not unlike a commodious beer-mug. From the 1460s trunnions had come into use and even the heavier pieces were being equipped with wheeled carriages. Elevating the barrel for ranging was achieved by the use of wedges.

Transportation was an area of major difficulty. Large teams of draught horses or oxen were required, a section of pioneers had to be added to the train, their task to level and fill the generally appalling roads over which the guns must pass. Larger pieces were still manufactured on the hoop and stave principle (hence the term 'barrel'), though casting in bronze was, by mid-century, commonplace. Another arm, growing in significance and potency, was the smaller handgun or 'gonne', which would soon become predominant and surpass the mighty war bow.

It was one thing to drag the great guns to fixed positions and batter castle walls; the handling of field artillery was an altogether different matter. Using lighter guns on the field was a relative innovation. Flodden was the first British battle in which the deployment of field artillery was to have a marked effect upon the outcome. Even that earnest advocate of modernity, Machiavelli has little faith. He regarded guns on the field as being more of a distraction, soon prone to being knocked out by enemy cavalry. The Italian cites the Swiss as the very model of steadfastness under fire; 'they never decline an engagement out of fear of artillery'.

In this he was overly contemptuous. During Bull Talbot's last doomed battle at Castillon as the Hundred Years War closed in 1453, the English had been badly mauled by guns firing from redoubts. The Lancastrians attempted similar tactics at Northampton seven years later but were foiled by a mix of torrential rain and treachery. Flodden would be the first fight in Britain to begin with an artillery duel as opposed to an archery exchange. The Earl of Warwick had deployed guns at Barnet but his efforts were frustrated by mist. His rolling, roaring cannonade which thundered blindly through the long hours of darkness did little but to rob those on both sides of rest.

Cast in Flanders, possibly around 1460, a notable survivor from this period is the great bombard 'Mons Meg'. The huge barrel is 3.95m in length and the bore measures 487cm. It threw a shot weighing some 549 lb, which is reputed to have carried for a full two miles. A tempting, if unlikely, legend asserts that the gun was cast by Molise McKim the hereditary smith of Threave and that the weapon was named after his ferociously tongued wife!

Part of the particular fascination of Flodden lies in the nature of that opening gun duel and the subsequent debate as to why the English fire proved so superior. That armies of the day employed a whole range of artillery pieces is beyond doubt. An inventory

Mons Meg on display in the 1680's. (Roger Griffith, Domestic Annals of Scotland. R. Chambers 1885, Wikimedia Commons)

compiled by Sir John Paston after the seizure of Caistor castle, listing the defenders' ordnance specifies:

> Two guns with eight chambers shooting a stone seven inches thick, twenty inches compass. Two lesser guns with eight chambers shooting a stone five inches thick, fifteen inches compass. Three fowlers shooting a stone twelve inches in compass; two short guns for ships with six chambers. Two small serpentines to shoot lead pellets; four guns lying in stocks to shoot lead pellets; seven handguns with other equipment belonging to said guns.

The Lord Treasurer's list provides details of the Scottish guns taken in the wake of the disaster at Flodden. The heavier *courtaulds* or more tellingly named *murtherers* weighed in at 6.000 lb with a 6½ inch bore throwing a 33½–36 lb shot. A large cast culverin was of similar weight but longer barrelled and thus of smaller bore. The lighter *sakers* weighed some 2,850 lb, throwing a 10 lb ball, cast bronze *culverin moyanes* were far lighter still, at some 1,500 lb, of 2 ½ inches bore and throwing a 5 lb ball. A number of smaller *falcons* were recovered and these are described as breech loaders.

It would seem likely that, whilst the handier pieces were mounted on wheeled carriages, bigger ordnance may still have been laid on fixed platforms. We know that two heavier guns were carried by cart from Threave to join the train and that cranage was employed to move the barrel from transport to firing platform. Given the rapidity with which all were moved prior to action, it would nonetheless seem reasonable that all were then mounted on carriages. The heavier guns required teams of three dozen oxen, medium sixteen oxen and a single horse, the lighter pieces eight oxen and a solitary horse. It seems most likely that these single horses were placed between the shafts of the carriage.

In July 1513, a larger piece was transported from Glasgow, en route to service in Ireland. This necessitated six carts with thirty-six draught horses, accompanied by eight 'close' carts, each transporting a single barrel of powder and a further pair laden with gun-stones weighing 33½ lb. The train that accompanied James included thirteen transport wagons, each laden with four barrels of blackpowder and twenty-eight draught animals loaded with shot crammed into panniers or creels.

One Ottoman monster in the care of Royal Armouries in Leeds is a cast bronze leviathan, manufactured in two halves then threaded together. Each section weights a full eight tons and the gun threw a stone ball weighing 670 lb! So effective was this massive ordnance it remained in service, guarding the Dardanelles for a full four centuries!

In recent years, Royal Armouries has experimented with Tudor guns of the post Flodden era, inspired by those found in the wreck of the *Mary Rose.* They aimed to construct a working replica of an older style gun, constructed of wrought iron staves and hoops. An expert blacksmith and team carried out this work which relied upon as many historic methods and tools as was practicable (evidence suggests Tudor smiths did use water-driven trip hammers). The staves, nine in all, were heated and carefully beaten into shape around a solid timber core and held in place by temporary clamps. A series of wrought-iron hoops and rings were then fashioned and hammer welded, laid on heated so as to contract to a snug fit. Placed alternatively the rings would take up the entire length of the barrel and were fitted with the staves and core in a vertical position.

The finished barrel with simple sighting ring foremost was fitted and lashed to a timber wheeled carriage and moved onto a range for test firing. Loading was from the breech and not muzzle, as was indeed commonplace. The wrought iron 'beer-jug' breech-block was part-filled with powder, topped with sawdust and straw, wadded and then sealed with a timber bung. The beauty of this arrangement was that several chambers could be kept loaded to permit rapid fire and loading at the breech was far safer.

Once the first projectile, lantern shot in this case, was loaded then the block was lifted into position (a substantial effort and four crewmen were required). The block is furnished with lifting rings and timber staves used to facilitate lifting. The first blast, effectively of grape, shredded a timber target and the death-dealing potential of lantern shot at close range was amply evidenced.

Next, solid shot, a stone ball from *Mary Rose* was fired. The weapon was aimed using the simple sight and elevated by means of a timber post and cross pin. To effect a tight seal at the breech the jug was buttressed with a timber forelock and then squeezed tight by an additional iron wedge. The ball easily punched through oak planking intended to match that of a man o'war. A vast cloud of smoke accompanied each discharge and we can easily envisage how the field would very quickly become shrouded in a dense blanket.

We are offered a valuable contemporary glimpse into guns, gun-making and the Scottish train in the campaign by the Accounts of the Lord High Treasurer. These record that, in the July, James had received a dozen cartloads of 'harnes(s)' from Denmark. John Barton had brought the king a handgun as early as 1507 and James was clearly fascinated, echoing the example of his unfortunate grandfather. At the outset it appears that most of the experts employed were continental immigrants, such as the 'French gunner' who was paid a handsome £3 10s per month. This was rather more than his Scottish comrades though rather less than those Flemings also in the king's service.

From 1508 onwards the Scots were casting guns at both Stirling and, latterly Edinburgh. One Alexander Bow, an Edinburgh potter, was placed in funds to the amount of £5.00 to buy metals for casting. Within a very short time, this sum had swollen to £65.00. Whilst Stirling was the first manufacturing centre to get underway, Edinburgh swiftly became the more important. The king's obsession with firepower continued. We are told, in the accounts, of his setting up targets in the Abbey Close (doubtless to the great alarm of the Abbot).

We also know that powder was being milled at the same time. We can further deduce from subsequent entries that the king had sourced canvas, six ells (137cm) of the fabric, to fashion into suitable targets 'quhilk the king schot gunnies at.' James also experimented by using guns for stalking 'ane deir.' These handguns clearly proved a favourite for we have records of the king commissioning several more at prices varying from £4.00–£10.00.

This superb train which James had amassed was comprised of five heavy siege pieces, curtals, throwing a 60-lb shot, two 18-pounder culverins, four 6-pounders 'culverins pikmoyenne' or 'sakers' and half a dozen 'culverins moyenne', larger versions of English 'serpentines'. Each of these great guns had its team of master gunner, matrosses and drivers, assisted by detachments of pioneers. In charge was Robert Borthwick, the king's proficient gunnery expert and *master meltar* (see appendix v), though a number of his more experienced crews had been detached for service with the fleet and the complement made up from men of lesser capability.

On 22 August, the main Scots army crossed the Tweed at Coldstream. Estimates of their numbers vary considerably. Allowing for the inevitable minor casualties, sick list and desertions beforehand, it may be that the army which crossed the Tweed numbered over forty thousand, still an awful lot. The first night was spent encamped by Twizelhaugh, the army's flanks protected by the waters of both Tweed and Till. The taking of Norham Castle was the Scots first objective. The castellan, John Anislow, believed himself ready, sure his garrison could hold out until the Earl of Surrey arrived with a relief force. He was wrong.

Built in the early 12th century by Bishop Flambard as a timber motte and bailey, the great stone bastion which was raised on the site by Bishop Hugh de Puisset, one of the most prolific builders amongst the Prince Bishops, comprised both inner and outer baileys, the latter defended by a moat. Much of this early work, particularly the enormous pile of the great keep, survived later alterations. The site itself forms a superb defensive location, standing high above the steeply rising banks of Tweed, dwarfing the pleasant settlement below, latterly immortalised in luminous oils by Turner. The original western gatehouse was sealed up at one stage but opened in the 15th century when a barbican was added.

Norham had withstood a series of earlier sieges, most recently 1497 and its defenders remained confident. This was misplaced. For the great fortress was essentially of medieval construction, ill-suited to withstand bombardment and so great a train as King James was bringing had never before been seen on the border. Anislow, the castellan, had confidently bragged to Surrey that 'he prayed God that the king of Scots would come with his puissance [power]' for he could defend the castle indefinitely 'till the time that the king of England came from France to its relief.'

This braggadocio reassured Surrey who was anxious not to hazard such a vital fortress – which 'answer rejoiced the earl much'. Regrettably so, for the English castellan was rather over optimistic in his assessment, even though Bishop Ruthin had steadily been building up reserves of powder and shot. This reassurance dissuaded Surrey from marching directly northward for, had Anisole appeared less certain, the earl would have ensured, as he had sixteen years prior, that the relief of Norham became his first priority.

Scottish batteries were initially laid at Lady Kirk bank on the north side of the Tweed. Their weight of shot vastly exceeded that available to the besiegers in 1497. These great guns pulverised the western gatehouse and punched a breach through a length of curtain wall running parallel to the river. With the Gunners declaring the gap 'practicable', the fortress was then subjected to infantry assault. Though the attackers took the outer ward their attempts on the inner ring were repulsed. James was anxious to secure the prize. Perhaps, here, we see evidence of his inexperience, launching costly attacks and squandering lives when the business was best left to his gunners.

Ancient walls, the great square keep rising above, were wreathed in smoke, acrid sulphurous odours choking damp summer air. Waves of Scottish foot, long pikes levelled, would be flung into the breaches. Their gunners would aim to collapse the wall from the base and outwards so clattering rubble formed a ramp for the foot. For their part the defenders would try and seal off the entry as soon as possible and defend the gap with every ounce of resolve. It would be bloody and exhausting work for both sides, broken stones soon slippery with spilled blood.

Nonetheless, after five days of intensive bombardment and three major attacks 'three great assaults three days together', the garrison found themselves critically short of powder and missiles. Anislow, on 29 August, felt obliged to throw in the towel whilst his men could still expect the courtesies of war.

Tudor chronicler Edward Hall believed Anislow's profligacy with his ammunition stocks was to blame for the disaster: 'he spent vainly so much of his ordnance, bows and arrows and other munitions that at the last he lacked, and so was, on the sixth day, compelled to yield upon the King's mercy.' The defeated castellan found himself a prisoner of war, packed off to Falkland Palace in Fife whilst the victorious Scots stripped his former charge with all of their customary zeal and thoroughness. Furniture, tapestries and liquor; all spoils went to the victors.

Norham was a long sought-after prize and its fall exposed the whole eastern flank of North Northumberland. The fortress was stripped and sacked but not slighted. For Surrey, this was both a disaster and humiliation. Norham was the key to the marches, its fall left the door wide open and enabled James to ravage North Northumberland at will '… this chance was more sorrowful to the Earl [of Surrey] than to the Bishop [of Durham], owner of the same.' The Bishop did write to Wolsey, however, averring that his grief was inconsolable. The compensation probably helped.

And that was pretty much it really. Norham's fall meant the whole defence scheme for the northern frontier, effective for centuries, had now collapsed. Berwick that moveable fortress, having changed hands fourteen times before 1482, stayed English. In Elizabeth's reign it would receive a massive state-of-the-art makeover but it would never be a castle again and the old castle beyond the new walls decayed until the advent of railways finally swept it away altogether.

From now on gentlemen would be building houses rather than bunkers though numerous border towers like Belsay or Dilston had a Jacobethan wing added on, tacked onto the old tower just in case. The Radcliffe Earls of Derwentwater threw up a fine and extensive mansion that completely enveloped the old hall tower at Dilston – though it has survived and the fine house has gone. But that's another story.

CHAPTER 5

→→→ → →→→ → →→→ → →→→ →

RAIDS AND REIVERS – A TROUBLED FRONTIER

1500–1600

Wha daur meddle wi' me?[1]
Wha daur meddle wi' me?
My name is little Jock Elliot,
And wha daur meddle wi' me?

WHEN ENGLAND AND SCOTLAND WERE AT LAST UNITED UNDER A SINGLE CROWN IN 1603, these two countries had been at war, outright or simmering, for three hundred years; since the time of William Wallace and the Wars of Independence which had kicked off in 1296. During the 16th century there were times of intense, open warfare between the two. Scotland had long been an ally of England's old enemy, France.

Indeed, in 1512 the 'Auld Alliance' between these two countries was extended, and all nationals of Scotland and France also became nationals of each other's countries, a status not repealed in France until 1903. In the following year (1513) this allegiance obliged James IV of Scotland to attack the English in support of his French allies, who had been attacked by Henry VIII. The result was Flodden, in which the Scottish king, many

---

1   Less colloquially this means: *Nobody interferes with me with impunity.* The verse is anonymous but often associated with the Elliot family.

of his nobles and perhaps ten thousand men were killed – *The Flowers of the Forest* of the folk song.

And things did not improve over the century. After a period of regency, James V of Scotland succeeded his father and married a French noblewoman, Mary of Guise, mother of his only daughter, Mary. In 1542, James' rag tag army was soundly and humiliatingly trounced at the Battle of Solway Moss in another disastrous campaign against the English. He died shortly afterwards.

Henry VIII failed in his ensuing diplomatic and then military attempts to win the hand of James' young daughter Mary (to be Queen of Scots) for his son Edward (to be Edward VI) – the so-called *Rough Wooing* that continued into the regency that followed Henry's own death in 1547. Mary had been sent to France, aged five, as intended bride of the French Dauphin. She might have done rather better had she stayed there.

> The Border country … was the ring in which the champions met; armies marched and counter-marched and fought and fled across it; it was wasted and burned and despoiled, its people harried and robbed and slaughtered, on both sides, by both sides. Whatever the rights and wrongs, the Borderers were the people who bore the brunt; for almost 300 years, from the late thirteenth century to the middle of the sixteenth, they lived in a battlefield that stretched from the Solway to the North Sea.

This harsh land north *and* south of the Border was a region of 'riding names', groups held together by the most powerful of all bonds – blood. Thus, not only was Northumberland subject to cross-border incursions from the Scots, but also to inter-clan raiding. Indeed, the Border Line itself meant little to the reivers:

> The raiders from Bewcastle, from Tynedale and from Redesdale were as much a nuisance to their compatriots as was anyone from over the Border. Indeed, at the time compatriot meant nothing and the Border did not count for much, for men who had made the place too hot to hold them on one side would flee to kinsmen and friends on the other, being 'Scottish when they will and English at their pleasure'

Reivers – from a 19th Century print. (G Cattermole, Wikimedia Commons)

Reivers (from the Old English *rēafian* – to rob) were not all 'outlaws', although some of them most certainly were. They came from all classes and backgrounds, having in common the ability to ride and to fight and the need to survive in a hostile environment. Marauding reivers carried out cattle-thieving raids with impunity, both across the border and against their neighbours, knowing that the rule of law simply did not apply in their dales. It was an accepted way of life. Practising systematic thievery and wholesale destruction, they have the dubious distinction of bringing the word *bereaved* into the English language, as indeed they did *blackmail*, another innovative reiver practice.

> By the sixteenth century, robbery and blood feud had become virtually systematic, and that century saw the activities of the steel-bonneted Border riders – noble and simple, robber and lawman, soldier and farmer, outlaw and peasant – at their height.

In other words, this was not a few villains who were perpetually attacking their peace-loving countrymen. Theft was the principal business of everyone in the region. It was simply a way of subsisting during the reiving 'season' from late August to February (Candlemas) whenever weather and moonlight allowed: 'A foray might involve a dozen riders or half a thousand, with the graynes[2] active every night the weather allowed, the bright reivers' moon their guiding star. So important was this lunar conspiracy that the image appears in border heraldry – the Scott's badge was a star and two crescent moons; mottoes such as 'we'll have moonlight again' were popular amongst riding names.'

By the middle of the 16th century life in the south of England was becoming relatively safe and prosperous. The Borders, by contrast, were fastened in the bitter grip of low intensity (when it was not high) warfare. Families in the area began to replace their old steadings, made of timber and earth, with relatively strong buildings made of stone. Indeed, the availability of local material was one reason that the mini castle, the bastle caught on. On the whole it was fairly well-off tenants who undertook this work rather than landlords – after all, it was their families and cattle that were under threat.

These new, defensible farmhouses were known as *bastles*, presumably from the French *bâtir* to build, as in *bastille*, a fortified building. The unruly and anarchic society in the Borders meant that the unification of the Crown in 1603 did not completely remove the need for them – the bastle continued to be built for many years. Roughly speaking, most were constructed between 1550 and 1650. Many bear a later date – which is the date of *renovation* rather than that of original construction.

They were not isolated structures. Many had outbuildings, the remains of which can often be seen (as at Black Middens in Tarset), and they were often built in sight of other bastles – indeed they are often found in small groups. This would facilitate an alarm being raised and would enable those being attacked to get instant backup from neighbours.

---

2 Grayne = a family or surname, e.g. Elliotts, Armstrongs.

Black Middens Bastle House. (Les Hull, Wikimedia Commons, CC BY-SA 2.0)

Complex as they are to construct, the **spiral** is a common form of castle/tower stairway. They have the great advantage of being both compact and eminently defensible. When the family was famously (or notoriously) left-handed such as the Scottish Kers, it is said the spiral stairs in their towers all have a left-hand twist so as to favour a ker-handed swordsman retreating upward.

Evistones town-ship, near Otterburn, is a superb example of a community of bastles. Some were extended, a second building being built onto the end of a first, at the 'byre door end', forming a larger whole. In other cases, they were built in terraces, as seems to have been the case at Wall village. There, individual bastles kept their integrity although they were linked to their neighbours – 'link' as opposed to 'executive' bunkers.

This may be a good place to point out that some bastles are known as *peles* or *peels* – Thropton Peel is an example. The words are often used synonymously, but the etymology of *peel* is from the French *pel*, meaning wooden stake. Bastles were defensible farmhouses; as such they are neither glamorous nor pretentious. Stark, rough hewn, they stand as firm as if they had sprung organically from the harsh upland itself. Utilitarian and austere, their allure (if they can claim such) arises from a perceived romance and durability.

On the ground floor was the barn or byre, into which cattle were driven when a raid was imminent or during particularly bad weather. Without drainage or stalls, it seems unlikely that this space was to be utilised for lengthy periods. Above lay the family's Spartan living quarters, devoid of comfort other than a fireplace set into one gable (usually at the opposite end to the doorway). Rarely bigger than 12m x 8m, bastles are rectangular in shape and typically have walls between 0.7m and 1.4m thick. Constructed of large, irregular stone blocks; gaps between the blocks were packed with smaller stones set in mortar. They have steeply pitched gables and many were probably roofed initially with heather thatching.

But are these castles? They're pretty unique and are built more by yeoman farmers than minor gentry. They fulfil the dictionary definition, people lived there and they're certainly fortified. They are a different type of military and social solution than motte and bailey; there's no statement of power or position. They were, in fact, a purely functional response to a particular problem.

What we lack is a Samuel Pepys, or Mrs. Pepys of the border. We hear about the reivers rather than hearing from them. How the goodwife felt about her husband's nocturnal enterprise is generally unrecorded. Domestic life, of course did go on, people married, often in defiance of a cross-border prohibition, raised children and focused on the daily business of survival. The women of Redesdale are as notorious as their men, riding out in their own right when necessary. Those remaining in the castle could and did act in defence of home and property, using gun, bow or knife to fend off intruders. Or sending out the raiders themselves. A famous 19th-century painting shows a goodwife presenting a pair of spurs on an empty platter. *Fetch the supper in.*

This is a militarised society but it also an agricultural one. Women work hard, tending animals, growing what vegetables and grain will thrive on land as poor as this and collecting whatever food is available. Wild herbs and greens collected in the spring provide much needed vitamins during the hungry gap before the garden crops come through. Later in the year, meat, poultry and fish traded in from the coast or plundered from the rivers need to be preserved ready for winter.

Grain – oats and barley mostly, for this is not wheat growing territory, will be ground into bread-flour. In times of greatest need all will eat the horse bread which takes its name from the cereals fed to animals: dried peas, oats and barley used to make a loaf of high density and legendary keeping qualities.

The same grains are the basis of that other staple, pottage. This is a thick soup/stew which simmers away on the back of the fire turning anything available into a savoury main dish eaten by all. Meat if you have any, grains and pulses, vegetables and herbs: in they all go. By March it is mostly water, left over barley and dried nettles. Unless the idle man of the house has managed to acquire a sheep or two. Mutton broth – the smell alone will fill a hungry stomach.

When we speak of the Border we are referring to a remote part of England, far away from the centre of power, difficult and expensive to police. A fairly complex means of trying to keep order was established as early as 1249, when both Scottish and English governments agreed that the border should be divided into six Marches – three on each side: East, Middle and West. From 1297 these Marches were controlled judicially and militarily by March Wardens. These officers were usually appointed from the south of the country, in order to avoid the obvious possibility of bias for or against the feuding *names* over which they were intended to hold sway. The examples of Percy and Neville in the 15th century evidenced the risks attached to conferring such vice-regal powers on unruly local magnates.

It was the Wardens' duty to see that peace was maintained, to administer justice and to deal with 'bills' or complaints. Backed up by a staff of deputies, captains and troopers, they tried with varying degrees of success to administer good law, but in doing so would frequently create personal enemies (some were murdered) and further bitterness between already bellicose riding names. They frequently caused more problems than they solved and most certainly did not implement peace and safety for the marchers. One such Warden was the notorious Sir John Forster; not from the south, we're proud to say but a native Northumbrian:

> A regular subject of Border correspondence, he was the target of frequent accusations ranging from collusion with the Scots and neglect of duty, to using his office as a cloak for thieving and skullduggery, his accusers further adding that Sir John's catalogue of shortcomings 'would fill a large book'. Most of this was in fact true and his protestations of innocence are somewhat less than convincing.

After a raid, with the lifting of cattle and possibly taking of lives, the thieves would naturally set off for the relative safety of tower or sheltering moss without delay. Above all else, success would lie in the speed with which sortie and getaway were accomplished. Escaping reivers would be much hampered by the four-legged spoils – cattle are notoriously difficult to move at speed. It was essential to be familiar with every step and inch of the landscape so that temporary lying up places and strategic sites for ambush were known and could be used with facility.

He who was left victim of such a raid had three choices: to make complaint to the Warden, to bide his time until he could wreak revenge (with interest if possible), or to mount a 'hot trod'. If some time elapsed before the pursuers set out it was known as a 'cold trod'. Either way, the legality of the trod depended on its being within six days of the raid. As George MacDonald Fraser points out, 'a careful line was drawn, under Border law, between a trod and reprisal raid'.

If the trod was cross-Border, it was essential to make it clear that legal pursuit was underway: a lighted turf was to be clearly visible on the pursuer's lance point, 'an earnest of open and peaceful intentions'. He had a legal right to assistance from marchers across the Border, and trying to hinder the trod was a punishable offence, one far more honoured in the breach than the observance.

The trod could easily involve a scrap; however strict the supposed rules, the business might frequently ended in a fierce skirmish during which fighters from either side stood to lose life or limb; 'the law was not likely to call a trod-follower to account if his rage got the better of him and he dispatched a reiver out of hand.'

A reiver looked nothing like a traditional knight in plate harness. As a specialist he needed the right gear to support such a dangerous business. First, and most importantly perhaps, he required a horse.

No steel or tubular **scaffolding** existed in the Middle Ages, scaffolds were constructed from timber. The platforms went up with the height of the building, some were, as today, free standing. More often the scaffold was supported by the finished sections of masonry, projected from timber lugs or putlogs – the sockets for these were left by masons as they laid the stones. Sometimes a round tower would be built using a spiral scaffold that wound around the rising walls. This served as a means of ferrying up mortar and materials while the width of the completed wall sections served as a working platform.

Remembering that the Borderers could be called up to fight for king and country (never with any marked enthusiasm), horses needed to be suitable mounts both for light cavalry work in time of war, and for raiding in time of ostensible peace. Known as *hobblers*, *hobilars* or *garrons*, they were sturdy and fast, and, like Cumbria's hardy Herdwick sheep, they were cheap to keep. There is evidence that they were not groomed and did not have need of shoes. They were said to be capable of 'transporting a man from Tynedale to Teviotdale and back in 24 hours'.

What was already bad enough was made even worse by the savage code of the vendetta, a relentless legacy of murder known as the 'feid' (feud). The inhabitants of southern Europe would have nothing to teach the borderers when it came to seeking revenge.

From Carter Bar, the high watershed that once divided two kingdoms, the view stretches northward over the rolling crests of Philip Law, Woden Law and Whitestone Hill. A sea of harsh grass and heather, plucked and furred by the winds in winter, a carpet of green in spring and summer. Secretive still and unspoilt: the border country offers the visitor unique insight into a troubled past.

Thirlwall Castle

History is a continuum and few places illustrate that as well as Thirlwall Castle. A 13th-century hall tower (first mentioned in 1255), it sits on a rocky knoll ten metres or so above the Tipalt Burn, covering the strategic Irthing Gap. Situated nicely between the wall forts of Aesica and Camboglanna, the Gap always mattered. It is built from stones lifted from Hadrian's work and, by a fine stoke of historical irony, the old tower was quarried to provide masonry for the adjacent 19th-century farm.

Longshanks appears to have bivouacked there with the De Thirlwalls. They were a robust bunch of Anglo Normans, active during the Scottish wars (one of them goes down fighting against Jamie Douglas in 1307, see following chapter). For a time in the 11th century, the king of Scotland was de Thirlwall's feudal superior. We know he heard a case in 1279 where the baron was in dispute with the Prioress of Lambley, one of those nasty litigious matters, excitingly set to be settled with trial by combat. De Thirwall's reputation was enough to overawe the lady's champion. The Prioress agreed to pay damages.

Later Thirlwalls fought in Edward III French wars and one, giving evidence in 1385 before Richard II, stated his father's age as 145! During the Three Hundred Years Border War, the Thirlwalls lived like robber barons. One, in the mid-14th century (possibly the greybeard referred to above), earned a particularly bad reputation, using his commission as licence to rob.

He kept a steward who was even worse, truly poisonous. Thirlwall had amassed quite a haul but his innumerable victims finally had enough and launched a major retaliatory strike. Once it was clear all was lost, the Steward chucked a heavy sack of valuables down the well and jumped in after. No surrender for him. He collapsed the shaft as he plummeted – the loot was buried forever. People have been hunting it ever since.

CHAPTER 6

➤➤➤ ⟶ ➤➤➤ ⟶ ➤➤➤ ⟶ ➤➤➤ ⟶

BIRNAM WOOD IS COME TO DUNSINANE – THE SCOTTISH EXPERIENCE

1500–1600

IF YOU WERE LOOKING FOR A FANTASY SCOTTISH TOWER HOUSE, Smailholm, just 8km west of Kelso, really is the business. It's a slender stone tower sitting on a small crag above a wee dark lochan. The sort of place you'd expect Scott to invent. Well, for once, he didn't have to – you could say Smailholm helped invent Scott.

The sickly boy was sent to spend summers in the bright clear air of his grandfather's farm just below the tower. No budding romantic could be unmoved – Smailholm appears in both *Eve of St John* and *Marmion*. Scott's uncle partially restored, certainly consolidated, what was then a ruin. The great man of letters brought the great man of art, Turner, to see the place. Happily, you can still see Smailholm today; the site is superbly conserved and maintained by Historic Scotland.

Move north and west onto that magical coast. Should you drive along the line of the present A816, heading from Oban and passing by the southern tip of Loch Awe, through Kilmichael and Kilmartin, then you have entered an enchanted landscape

Smailholm Tower. (Dave souza, Wikimedia Commons, CC BY-SA 2.5)

where echoes of the distant past resonate as steady as beat of drum. Rearing up from the plain, on the right hand, just before you pass the churchyard of Kilmachumaig, is the great hill fort of Dunadd, mighty, rock-hewn fortress and capital of *Dalriada* ('*Riada*'s Portion'). For centuries it dominated the ground and withstood the repeated assaults of hostile Pictish tribes.

A stiff scramble up the conical mound brings you to twin plateaux on the summit. On the narrow spur between these two lies the 'Inauguration Stone' – the outline of a human foot incised into the rock. Nearby, is a shallow basin cut from the stone with a boar in relief. It was here that ancient kings were consecrated, each slipping his bare foot into the carving, a symbolic affirmation that the new ruler would tread the same paths as his forbears. A scene atmospherically recreated in Polanski's *Macbeth.*

As to the image of the boar – its exact function isn't clear though the basin appears to have been used for ritual ablutions. With outstanding views along Kilmartin Glen and the serpentine trail of the River Add, the place vibrates with the pulse of history.

The citadel echoes the cyclopean masonry of the Bronze Age settlements of Homeric Greece, great Mycenae, Tiryns and Argos. This isn't strictly a castle though it comes pretty close, an early castle perhaps. It was the stronghold of a petty king or chieftain but it served the same purpose – to overawe restless natives, deter trespassers and provide a base for offensive operations.

Medieval Scotland, as Marc Morris ably points out, has a pretty bad reputation for gratuitous violence and indeed there was a lot of it about. Ask Lady MacDuff. In part this reputation was deserved. There was a lot of scrapping, murder, flourishing vendettas and general mayhem. It wasn't necessarily *all* bad and the Scots did have the English to contend with. In general terms royal authority was never as tight as in England, all those wild glens beyond the highland line and the even wilder borders were frequently lawless. Kings of Scotland didn't have anywhere near as secure a revenue stream as their southern counterparts and were frequently bedevilled by minority kingships dominated by fractious and self-seeking regency councils.

Having spent so much of his early life in England, David I, when he at last came into his own, brought with back with him a vanguard of ambitious Normans (though it was probably Macbeth who'd first imported them as mercenaries. Names such as Moreville, Soulis, Lindsay, Somerville and Bruce brought their motte building habits with them. As soldiers, they were the ideal instrument for stamping the new king's authority over the wild northern shires. Soon mottes sprang up at Duffus near Elgin, Inverurie in the Garioch and at Invernochty near Braemar. This wasn't conquest, it was infiltration. But these Normans were just as acquisitive as those who'd followed Duke William in 1066 and began winning lands in Galloway and the south-west. Their mailed horsemen contemptuously crushed Somerled's caterans at Renfrew in 1164.

For some Scots, the 13th century represents a golden age in castle building, a golden age in general, before the dark abyss of the Wars of Independence. The last Norsemen were seen off

Caerlaverock Castle. (Simon Ledingham, Wikimedia Commons, CC BY-SA 2.0)

at the Battle of Largs and the economy was building. New and impressive stone castles were rising at Dirleton, Kildrummy, Bothwell and Caerlaverock, none of your timber mottes and baileys but superbly cut masonry with hefty drum towers, ranges of well-built domestic structures hugging their walls; castles of *enceinte*. In the dim, weird west royal power was nibbling away at the old Norse-Gael heartlands.

Dunstaffnage, on the shore of Loch Etive, north of Oban is a prime example and the exquisite Gothic chapel is the first of its kind to appear in Scotland. The very distinctive shapes of both Mingary and Tioram appear around this time. The approach is from the rock and shingle beach by the settlement at Kilchoan on the tip of the very long finger of Ardnamurchan. The castle rises like a movie set from a knoll overlooking the beach. It is perfect and there is nothing modern in sight. It could be any time from the 14th to 18th centuries. You're not supposed to work your way inside for reasons of health and safety. There is nobody there. Just the gulls circling raucous overhead, the thrum and heave of the restless sea and the odd passing ferry.

Possibly, or even probably, built by MacDougall or MacDonald of Ardnamurchan in the 13th century, overlooking the Sound of Mull and safeguarding the back door into Lochaber it had a fairly exciting history during the deadly era of the age of forays, after James IV had scrapped the moribund Lordship (Clan Donald disagreed). After the failure of the Armada in 1588, a Spanish galleon *San Juan de Sicilia* came aground on Mull. Maclean of Duart, not one to miss an opportunity, enlisted the survivors as auxiliaries in his fight with MacDonald. MacLean with his new friends had a crack at Mingary but was seen off after a short three-day battle. Next up was Alistair MacColla himself in 1644, who terrorised a covenanter garrison into surrendering.

Much of what you see today is 17th-century rebuilding when old castles were given makeovers as garrison outposts and barrack blocks or 'piles' replaced original buildings. These west coast castles are reminiscent of shell keeps. There is often a high curtain wall circling a small inner space and the buildings cluster together on the inside. They're impossibly beautiful and look like they've just sprung from the pages of Scott or Stevenson.

Not far from the base of the Ardnamurchan peninsula, the waters of Loch Moidart meet the river Shiel and have created a small archipelago, cut off at high tide and called Eilean Tioram or, less poetically, the Dry Island. Castle Tioram sits on the tiny islet. Some years ago having driven down the narrow road that winds through fairytale woodland, we broke free of the birches to see the castle, unfolding like a pop up picture from books long ago, the perfect blue of the loch behind. The tide was creeping in and we waded, knee deep over the shingle bar, the water energised by the peat, caressing pallid lowlanders calves like a primeval benediction. This place is also meant to be sealed off on safety grounds: we'd best say no more.

If you're after earthly paradise, on a fine day anyway, Tioram will do nicely. The foundation probably dates from the local anarchy after Somerled's death. The rather glorious Christina MacRuari, saviour of Bruce, possessed a fleet of galleys which gave her hegemony over the sea to Ireland. That proved very handy for Robert who needed all the help he could find. The high curtain wall is pentagonal and of 13th-century origin. Again it is reminiscent of a shell keep, early interior buildings were probably timber-framed.

Local legend insists it wasn't Christina but her niece, Amy, who built Tioram. Probably both traditions are partly true as Amy may have significantly rebuilt/re-modelled the earlier structure. She likely constructed the tower house, raised the wall height and crenellated the parapet. Her son Ranald became the first Chief of MacDonald of Clanranald, a line that ran and ran through the bloody day on Culloden Moor. The MacDonalds still owned Tioram until well into the 20th century.

When Alexander III took his fatal tumble in 1286, nobody could quite have foreseen what was to follow. The Wars of Independence were, from Longshanks' perspective, just a police action against a disobedient vassal who'd broken his oath. (Disappointingly for devotees of the *Braveheart* school, Edward never de-fenestrated anyone, that was Henry I). For the Scottish patriots the fight was about liberty and country. They would receive no mercy.

Kildrummy, near Alford in Aberdeenshire, is a superb castle, though now largely ruinous. The visitor centre has a fine model that gives you a glimpse of past glories. The castle was built in a 'D' shape with the long rear wall covered by a deep ravine. A pair of very strong round towers completed each end of this long section with smaller towers mid-way towards the large gatehouse. This was remodelled By Master James (who we last encountered in Wales) though Edward was already overspent and Scotland would never get the full treatment. The Snow Tower, larger of the two at the western extremity of the rear curtain, housed most of the domestic offices and followed the contemporary French style. This was then augmented by a sophisticated hall range built between the two grand towers.

In 1306, Longshanks laid siege to Kildrummy, energetically defended by King Robert's younger brother, Neil Bruce. Edward entrusted operations to his far less able son, then Prince of Wales. The defenders fought hard, why not, they knew there'd be no clemency. Kildrummy, if we believe the story, fell not to assault or even by starvation but through greed. Neil Bruce's blacksmith, a fellow called Osbourne, sold out to the English and as part of the deal, started a disastrous fire which destroyed most of the defenders' stores and compelled them to surrender. It was curtains for Neil but the treacherous smith got his just desserts too. It is said his reward of gold coins was melted down and poured red hot into his throat. Seems like a waste of bullion.

Two years earlier Longshanks had appeared before the walls of Stirling, held by a garrison barely 30 strong captained by Sir William Oliphant. The crushing of Wallace and his field forces at Falkirk in 1298 had swung the pendulum back in England's favour. Still, Stirling aloof on its high volcanic plug was a very tough nut indeed. But Edward had Master James. He was as expert in knocking castles down as he was in building them. The siege began that April and the Savoyard constructed a dozen powerful engines which deluged the stubborn defenders with a constant barrage of missiles, including it seems an early form of explosive mix.

Finally, Oliphant asked for terms but had to wait. Master James had put together a monstrous trebuchet, the wonderfully and aptly named Warwolf. Edward wanted to see his new toy in action. Oliphant and company simply had to hug their walls and endure the storm. Their endurance was rewarded: the playful king spared all their lives. Well, with one exception – a renegade Englishman who had made the wrong choice.

The Stewarts would rule from 1371 till 1688 (with a short interval provided by Oliver Cromwell). Their tenure was frequently weak and rarely happy. James I ascended as a minor, was held captive in England for most of his adolescence and died at the hands of his own nobility. James II, after feuding with the overmighty Douglases indulged his obsession with artillery once too often and was blown up when one if his own guns burst. James

III also inherited as a minor, ruled badly and was finally killed by his nobles. James IV did well enough till 9 September 1513 and Flodden Field. His son James V died of shame or malaise after repeating his father's mistake in 1542 and suffering an even more humiliating defeat. As for his daughter Mary; well we all know what happened to her. Her son James VI achieved a double first; he died in his bed and became King of England in 1603.

In fairness to the Stewarts (descendants of those Norman knights/carpet-baggers who came north with David I), Scotland wasn't an easy place to control. Along its entire length the west coast of the mainland is studded with the passages of long sea lochs. The land is often bare and rugged, steep, mist shrouded mountains rising inland. In such inhospitable terrain, with much life and industry on the islands, it is natural that the sea would offer the most attractive highway. The waters were often contested as Norse and Gael, then the later clan affinities, struggled to exert hegemony. In all Britain there is no other region so little changed by development. Since the dark epoch of the Clearances in the late 18th and 19th centuries, population has declined, many of the old settlements swept away, only the gaunt and abandoned walls, mute testimony to a largely vanished way of life, remain. Lots of castles, happily, have survived.

Guarding the coast

Coastal defence is as ancient as warfare. Changes in the nature of the perceived maritime threat govern the measure of response. The Dalriadic Scots built their forts, like Dunadd, close to the water's edge. Dumbarton Rock was the chief hold of Strathclyde. Somerled, the Norse-Gael Lord of the Isles, built a chain of forts to guard and victual the galleys patrolling the sea-lanes of the West and these formed the foundation of many coastal castles, Dunaverty, Mingary and Tioram. Others like Tantallon, Dunbar, Berwick and Eyemouth frequently featured in the long wars with England. During the Napoleonic era, when the possible threat of

French invasion hung in the air, a new form of coastal defence, the Martello Tower, was conceived and thrown up around the nation's coastline. They're nice but they don't satisfy the devotee of the castle.

James VI described the ancient Kingdom of Fife as a 'beggar's mantle fringed with gold'. He was referring to the wealthy chain of coastal ports and fishing harbours. Though of course, St. Andrews also being justly famed as one of Europe's great universities. The ports traded with the Low Countries, exporting wool, linen, coal and salt. Southwards, across the Forth, the coastline of East Lothian is dominated by sweeping cliffs that fall, dazzlingly sheer to the sea, gaunt sentinel of the Bass Rock standing off. The bare remains of lonely Fast Castle (one of the most dramatic sites in Britain if you have a head for heights), still cling to their precarious outcrop. Meanwhile, Eyemouth retains traces of the defences constructed there in the 1540's by the French to counter the English strength at Berwick.

With their myriad inlets and harbours, the coasts of the western isles proved a haven for locals who sought to augment their meagre incomes by indulging in the more profitable game of piracy. The inhabitants of Canna proved so adept that the Abbot of Iona felt compelled to request a blanket excommunication for the offenders. Pabay, in the 16th century was a noted lair for outlaws who earned their living by preying on ships and neighbours. Longay, off Scalpay was another notorious haunt – in Gaelic the name means 'pirate ship'. The sea-spoilers took merchantmen and fishing vessels from Flemings, Scots and English, the lure of profit neatly transcending any nationalist sentiment.

These buccaneering tendencies were by no means the sole province of disadvantaged commons; the lure was equally attractive to cash-strapped gentry or any with an eye for profit. Alexander, the swashbuckling entirely disreputable Earl of Mar, victor of Harlaw, was happy to partner provost Davidson of Aberdeen in the 15th century. Later, in 1518, Calum Garbh Macleod ('Lusty Malcolm') established a base on Rona. Here was located a secret natural harbour, the *Port nan Robaireann*

Z Plan Castle: This was a form of Scottish tower house with a strong central tower flanked by two additional wings (sometimes later additions) set at diagonally opposite corners. The latter were studded with gun loops allowing the central block to be covered by fire from the wings. This is different from the L plan castle, again most commonly a Scottish feature, where the build is in the form of, on plan, an 'L'. This has the advantage that the projecting tower can provide cover to the main entrance – archers and, later, musketeers had a clear field of fire.

(literally, 'the Robbers' Port). From his stronghold of Brochel Castle, the MacLeod turned the various activities of individual sea-robbers into a flourishing, family enterprise.

One of the more notable sieges of the Wars of Independence involved the celebrated Countess of Dunbar, 'Black' Agnes. 'Black' because her lustrous hair was very dark. Agnes had a good patriotic pedigree. Her father, Thomas Randolph, Earl of Moray, was Bruce's nephew and a highly successful commander; her mother Isabel was a Stewart. She married Patrick, 9th Earl of Dunbar and March, a leading Scottish magnate, generally loyal when he wasn't being disloyal.

There's not much left of the great coastal fortress of Dunbar. Cromwell trashed the place (as he did many others), after he trashed the Scottish army in 1650. In 1338, whilst Agnes was in charge as chatelaine, an English force laid siege to the place. She only commanded a handful of defenders but was determined to fight: 'Of Scotland's King I haud my house, I pay him meat and fee, and I will keep my gude auld house, while my house will keep me.' To borrow from G. M. Fraser once again – 'sod off'.

The Earl of Salisbury, commanded the besiegers who let fly with a barrage of missiles delivered by a range of timber-built siege engines. This was probably more psychological than hopeful but Agnes refused to be cowed. She ostentatiously exposed herself on the battlements dusting the merlons after each projectile sheared off. This kind of theatre matters in a siege. The English responded by building a great siege tower or 'beffroi' which could overtop the walls and launch men at arms onto the parapet. Agnes' men managed to chuck a massive boulder down onto the tower wrecking the thing.

Archers on both sides tried to pick off targets of opportunity, a war of sniping. The Scots were decent shots and one of Salisbury's close companions was skewered next to him. 'Agnes' love shafts go straight to the heart', the earl joked, his knightly sangfroid undented. Salisbury resorted to bribery, usually a sound choice and paid off a junior Scottish officer to leave the postern open and unguarded. The canny Scot took the cash but reported straight back to Agnes. When the English commander led his men through the gate, the portcullis slammed down. Salisbury himself jumped back just in time though others were captured.

Having tried brute force, starvation and skulduggery, Salisbury fell back on terror, always a workable choice. He'd captured Agnes' brother John, Earl of Moray and threatened to string him up if his sister did not strike her colours. Agnes casually retorted that while she'd like to spare her sibling, she was not about to hand over the keys and if the unlucky John did swing, well than she'd gain an earldom of her own! In the event Moray was spared. One imagines Agnes knew Salisbury was bluffing; at least or you'd hope so.

As Dunbar is on the coast, completely encircling the castle and cutting off all means of supply wasn't easy. Salisbury was determined to try and did his best but Ramsay of Dalhousie managed to cram a company of reinforcements into small boats and run the blockade. He sneaked his men inside by the sea gate then promptly launched a raid on the English outposts, causing confusion and alarm. After five long months Salisbury conceded defeat and lifted the siege. It was one – nil to Agnes – 'Came I early, came I late, I found Agnes at the gate…'

Royal minorities were never good, invariably rival factions quarrelled and brawled. James II had a serious dislike of the all-powerful Douglases, all powerful and far too powerful. In 1440, in a scene straight from *Game of Thrones,* the ten-year-old king invited the 16-year-old 6th Earl of Douglas and his even younger brother to dinner at Edinburgh Castle. Thereafter known as the notorious 'Black Dinner' where both Douglas guests were savagely murdered after a mock trial. A dozen years later the king invited the 8th Earl Douglas to Stirling and personally stabbed him to death. James' dinner parties were clearly very lively affairs – one wonders if he ever had trouble filling the benches.

On the other hand, the Black Douglases were a pretty rough bunch. None was more feared than the aptly named Archibald the Grim. He was a bastard son of the famous James the 'Black' Douglas, Bruce's ferocious and able lieutenant. Archibald did well in the Scottish service – David II, in 1369, appointed him Lord of Galloway. With the death of the legitimate 2nd earl during the Battle of Otterburn in August 1388, Archibald scooped up the other Douglas lands and titles becoming 3rd earl, the most powerful man in Scotland.

Archibald served as West March Warden from 1361, eliminating the few remaining English outposts. Just over a decade later, he was able to exert control over the whole of Galloway. What he needed now was a really, really strong castle. Archibald might have been grim but he was also a realist. The more powerful he became the longer his list of enemies and it was a fair tally to start with.

Head up to pretty Castle Douglas in Dumfries, just 2.5km from the town, on an island in the River Dee, stands Threave. It's impressive, even though now just a ruined shell. You still need a boat to get onto the tiny island, rather bigger now than it was and it is a superb settling. Grim though just about covers it, there aren't any frills here.

Threave is likely the first true tower house built in Scotland, sometime in the 1370s. It is a big, solid keep-like structure 18.4m × 12.1m, originally five storeys high with access to the first-floor reception hall from a wooden stair tower as you came over a movable timber bridge. The basement could only be got to by ladder from above – its barrel-vaulted rooms were just for storage. Climbing a spiral stair set into the massively thick walls, you got to the grand hall. From there, if so privileged, to the Lord's accommodation above that with a garret for servants (or additional defenders), at the very top. It exudes strength and purpose.

What, we might ask, is the difference between a keep and a tower? Outwardly they look very similar but are, in fact, very different in specifics. The keep forms part of a wider defensive structure, a motte with attitude. People don't necessarily live there though; it's a last-chance bastion and symbol of power. The tower, every bit as mighty every bit as high in status, is still a residence and often has no wider defences other than a courtyard or barmkin wall.

Still, Threave looks businesslike rather than homely. Here was a man who knew he had enemies. As Marc Morris points out, Chris Tabraham's extensive excavations in the 1970s showed that just outside the castle there were separate high-status buildings, probably an ancillary hall and chapel. These were undefended and the island was home to a thriving township. Perhaps, in the late 14th century, it didn't really look all that unwelcoming.

Still, it was grim enough and soon got grimmer. Archibald's glittering career was really the zenith of Douglas' power. In the following century, the 8th Earl, before being done in by James (the earl himself was no angel), had extended the defences quite dramatically. He added an artillery 'house' or curtain, studded with gun loops and bolstered by three stubby towers. He also added a defensive wall on the river bank. The artillery provision is the first of its kind in Britain and shows the earl was expecting trouble. Which arrived.

His successor the 9th earl finished the artillery house and added earthworks north of the tower. His civil war against the king ended in defeat at Arkinholm in May 1455. One by one his castles fell till only Threave held out. The king came to lay siege to it that June. It is said he dragged the great bombard Mons Meg overland to blast the place. This proved difficult. The castle held out for two intense months till the king abandoned might for money and effectively bribed the garrison into surrender. In 1640 during the Bishops' Wars a royalist force held out for thirteen weeks and the vengeful covenanters wrecked the place to avoid a repeat. What we see today is what they left. It's still big and still grim though.

By 1493, the MacDonald Lordship of the Isles was pretty much played out and James IV scrapped the title to assume direct rule of the highlands and islands. This seemed like a good idea, using other magnates such as Huntly and Argyll as more malleable surrogates. However, the collapse of Clan Donald's hegemony led to chaos rather than control. By 1503, disturbances had become widespread and Huntly was engaged in wholesale dispossessions of those who refused to submit. With Clan Donald's surviving agitator, Donald Dubh. Lending legitimacy to their cause (old John of the Isles died in January 1504), the rebels under Torquil Macleod struck back. The Isle of Bute, an earlier target, was again extensively despoiled

Parliament, sitting in March 1504, commissioned Huntly to retrieve Eilean Donan and Strome castles, whilst a naval command, assembled under the ever-vigilant eye of Sir Andrew Wood (a hugely successful privateer), was entrusted to the Earl of Arran. This fleet was to take the rebels' stronghold of *Cairn na Burgh*, west of Mull in the Isles of Treshnish. The castle, a fair bit of which survives, unusually straddles two small islands, called, in Gaelic, *Cairn na Burgh Mor Cairn na Burgh Beag*.

The King's naval squadron, with a full complement of heavy cannon, soon proved its worth. Accurate gunnery swiftly flattened *Cairn na Burgh*. Few details of the siege have survived but the operation would clearly have been a difficult one. The ships had to come in as close as the waters permitted and deliver regular broadsides, operating essentially floating batteries. It's uncertain how many guns the rebels had but nowhere near enough. Several chiefs; Maclean of Lochbuie, MacQuarrie of Ulva and MacNeil of Barra found themselves in irons. Gradually the power and authority of the crown was restored. But the west still simmered and would go on simmering for generations.

Eilean Donan Castle; pitched on a tiny tidal islet where three long-fingered sea lochs meet was, in historic terms, the frontier between Lords of the Isles and the Earls of Ross. The castle began life on a larger scale in the 13th century when a longer curtain wall enclosed virtually the whole of the available surface. A tower house went up in the next century and the walls shrank to pretty much their current positions with more defences added on the eastern flank. By then it belonged to Clan Mackenzie and last saw action during the Jacobite alarum of 1719. As it had been used as a rebel base, the Royal Navy made a point of blasting the walls to smithereens.

What exists today is the third most visited castle in Scotland after Edinburgh and Stirling. It was rebuilt from scratch by Lieutenant-Colonel John MacRae-Gilstrap between 1919 and 1932, a post Great War catharsis and a monument to all those clansmen who didn't come back. It came into public ownership in 1955 and now attracts over 300,000 visitors annually.

Eilean Donan. (Author's own, courtesy of Adam Barr (Adamski))

By the dark waters of Loch Assynt in Sutherland on an empty shore, the lone finger of a broken tower rises in a kind of mute supplication. Once, half a century back, the half-ruined vaulted basement was crammed with Georgian naval guns. This is Ardvreck Castle or what is left of it. Nobody seems to care as though something bad hangs over the place. And yes, there's a reason for that.

In 1650, the Paladin Montrose had come back for a final effort. He should have stayed away. The magic was gone and comebacks tend to go badly. New King Charles II used him and then discarded him. The marquis' final expedition was a pale shadow of his earlier prodigies and ended in ignominious rout. He was on the run in the bitter, barren wastes of Sutherland. Ardvreck was the seat of Neil Macleod of Assynt. Neil was Seaforth's man and had served earlier under Montrose at Inverness. The laird's attractive young wife took the celebrity fugitive and a Major Sinclair in. Macleod undertook to hide his guests, feed and clothe them, then see to their safe onward passage.

This was a significant burden but the rule of hospitality, once offered, was inviolate. Unfortunately, Neil was in debt, his lands heavily mortgaged. It was the wife, the new Lady Macbeth in this latter-day tragedy, who pointed out how useful the government's reward of £25,000 might prove in such straitened circumstances. It was a huge sum and greed got the better of honour. Macleod's ghillie set off for the garrison at Tain even as he was offering the fugitives a restorative dram. That proved to be an end to the remarkable career of the Marquis of Montrose.

Callously abandoned by the king he had risked his life for, he was humiliated, tortured and killed by the vengeful covenanters. On 23 June Charles II landed and rode up the length of Canongate, the head of his father's greatest champion spiked above him. He probably didn't even look. Macleod failed to profit by his treachery: his disgusted neighbours trashed Ardvreck and husband and wife.

James Douglas, known as the 'Black' was one of Robert Bruce's most active supporters. In 1307, with Bruce on the run,

Douglas paid the price of loyalty. An English garrison sequestered his family seat at Douglas Castle and diverted his rents. The Scots king gave him authority to mount a raid on his own patch but could spare no men.

He called upon his old steward Thomas Dickson to muster a gang of tenantry keen to have a crack at the invader. The entire English garrison would attend mass on Sunday, everybody did. The volunteers, all locals, mingled with the unsuspecting English – all of whom were all killed or captured.

James and his merry band returned to his newly liberated castle to eat the meal already laid out. After dining and clearing out everything portable, he poisoned the well, spoiled the remaining stores, beheaded his terrified prisoners and added their headless corpses to the pile. He then set fire to the place. The event would become known as the Douglas Larder – a fine example of 'frightfulness' (terror). It was another atrocity in an atrocious war and a lesson to English squatters and freebooters that 'we know where you live'. The rule in this Anglo Scottish war was that there were no rules at all.

Black Douglas was not done. One of the Northumbrian Thirlwall's, was appointed to command a new English garrison at the Castle. This time Douglas used an old reivers' trick, sending in a squad to seize grazing cattle and draw the occupiers out into an ambush. Thirlwall took the bait which cost him and half his men their lives; the rest scattered back behind the walls.

Third time lucky for the English? Sir John of Webton was the new castellan. Sentries on the parapet spotted what seemed to be a slow-moving column of loaded hay wains, led by women. Just what they needed as fodder was running short. Sir John led a sally but the girls turned out to be boys (the sort who carry swords) with many more skulking in the woods. The English were routed and this time Douglas battered in the gates to capture all the survivors. In accordance with Bruce's doctrine Douglas then razed his own home to the ground. This was, after all, total war.

CHAPTER 7

THE LAST HUZZAH – CIVIL WARS

1640–51

PRESTON HALL MUSEUM NEAR STOCKTON-ON-TEES HOSTS GEORGES DE LA TOUR'S ENIGMATIC MASTERPIECE, *The Dice Players.* The artist depicts a group of soldiers, still in military dress, gambling by candlelight. Their kit suggests the era of the English Civil Wars (though, more likely, these are from the continent and the Thirty Years War). The men wear quality harness, are young and very intent. One well-dressed young woman watches from the sideline; a senior figure appears to preside.

This is not gaming. These ambitious officers are throwing dice to determine who shall lead the assault at dawn, who will risk his life with the 'forlorn hope', the post of maximum danger and greatest opportunity. No doubt a scene just like it was enacted in the Scottish camp drawn up outside the town and castle of Newcastle upon Tyne in October 1644. It was destined to be one of Britain's last great formal sieges.

The fight for Newcastle that autumn was, from the defenders' viewpoint, a battle largely without strategic purpose. Parliament needed to restore coal supplies to the capital. Without hope of relief the mayor John Marley could scarcely justify hanging on. Yet, by forcing the Scots to sit down before the walls, these troops were prevented from taking the offensive against the king and were made to expend vast resources for no gain. By holding out Marley denied vital coal supplies to the enemy.

By 7 August, the victors of Marston Moor were marching northwards. The marquis of Newcastle's proud brigade had been near annihilated. The noose was tightening but the Scots were short of supplies generally and, above all, of cash. As the Earl of Leven's army commenced its trek northwards, the Earl of Callendar had brought additional forces southward and was getting on with the job. On 27 July he stormed Gateshead on the south bank of the Tyne – held (weakly) by the Royalists.

Despite this initial success, the Chamberlain's accounts imply that the besieged were rather better provided for than their adversaries at this stage. Callendar had taken Sinclair's and the Earl Marischall's regiments over the Tyne to establish a bridgehead. He had also constructed a pontoon bridge east of Sandgate. Professor Terry places this just east of the Ouseburn where the topography would provide cover from any defender's guns – using a natural bend in the river and the higher ground between Pandon and Ouseburn. His inspection was harassed by fire from the walls and from an outlying sconce, the Shieldfield fort.

Once he'd arrived the Earl of Leven assumed overall command and set about tightening the vice. Callendar had extended his original blockade on the Gateshead side to encompass the eastern flank of the city; the two positions linked by an improvised and sheltered crossing. The Scottish chronicler and adventurer Lithgow relates that security for the bridge was entrusted to Kenmure's Regiment, strengthened by a series of three keels (coal carriers), roped together as a form of floating guardhouse.

It's likely that the low plateau, on which the church of St. Ann's now stands, formed a fire position for a further gun battery. Mining operations began around Sandgate. Leven was a believer in the efficacy of mining, a tactic as old as warfare itself. As the Scottish guns belched fire many of the inhabitants living close to the river were driven to find safety away from its banks.

Meanwhile the defenders had also been busy. Throwing stones were ready to be chucked from the walls, gaps between merlons had been filled with rubble and mortar. The gates were firmly closed, propped and barricaded. The old external ditch had been cleared and deepened, masonry plastered with a rough mix of

Late 16th-century illustration of cannon with gabions. (Ramelli, Agostino, 1531–c. 1600; Library of Congress/Wikimedia Commons)

slick, puddled clay. Various outbuildings and random structures which had been allowed to obscure the walls and impeded fields of fire were knocked down. It didn't really matter; Newcastle was a medieval fortress, its defences hopelessly obsolete.

Barbican – Newcastle Castle. (Author's own, courtesy of Adam Barr (Adamski))

Before all this huge labour had been expended, Leven had on 16 August, demanded the City surrender. It was all outwardly gentlemanly; Marley and the council returned an equal courteous response next day. These high sentiments masked the reality that the Scots were daily strengthening their positions and their inexorable grip which the defenders had the neither means nor prospects to resist. The suburbs, those not already burnt, were in their hands, their investiture complete.

Not all citizens shared Marley's fighting spirit. Several of the less determined Aldermen had slipped out and sought sanctuary in Sunderland. Leven had recruited a significant labour force comprised of three thousand colliers, keelmen (those who operated the keel boats) and general labourers. Ironically many of these men had been conscripted by Marlay to construct the defences. His refusal to pay them had caused huge resentment. Leven appears to have put rather more faith in mining operations than in his guns. The Royalists still had teeth though; on Saturday 20 August, the defenders sallied out to beat up the besiegers' quarters by Closegate. A couple of Scots were killed and more, including several officers, captured.

Daily the Scots extended their lines and burrowed furiously whilst the defenders' guns, most particularly those from the castle, kept up a steady barrage. Scots' General Baillie was concentrating his efforts against the great bulwark of Newgate, his guns most likely placed on the Leazes (an open area just outside the walls) from where they inflicted considerable damage, not just upon the walls but also to the fabric of St. Andrew's Church.

Here, by Leazes, mines were also creeping close to the walls. Baillie having enjoyed his lunch on the 24th, found his digestion disturbed by another sortie. The besiegers, with very few officers, put up a poor showing and just legged it. This was not encouraging.

By this time an increasingly serious threat was developing in Scotland itself as the Marquis of Montrose embarked upon his remarkable 'Year of Miracles'. Callendar and Lindsay were drawn off early in September, taking three cavalry and one infantry regiments north. Nonetheless, siege operations progressed. By 7 September Leven was predicting 'a short end of the work'. He was ever inclined to place more reliance on his sappers than his gunners.

Leven expressed this confidence in the text of a further eminently reasonable summons. To accompany these diplomatic overtures, leaflets inciting the citizens to lay down arms were scattered over the walls by the sackful. Marley returned a further courteous but stiffly defiant response. Brave words all round but the plain fact was that the vice was tightening and there was a growing body of opinion within the walls that favoured agreeing to terms.

David Leslie, at this time an energetic and capable cavalry officer, had bottled up the Royalists in Cumberland and Westmorland; no help could be expected from that quarter. For the Royalists in Newcastle, no other hope remained. Leven's response to Marley's defiance was to unleash Baillie's battery on the Leazes. It took three hours to bring down a section of wall, opening a practicable breach. No actual assault followed, he was just making a point. The defenders immediately filled the gap with improvised barricades.

Next Sunday, the Royalist sappers, engaging in counter-mining, discovered one of the Scots mines by Sandgate sunk closest to the river. Lithgow confirms a further three shafts were already being dug and Callendar (now returned) had the initial charge exploded to save the garrison from finishing the job by flooding the mine. Meanwhile the Scots officers continued to grouse over the lack of supplies, both rations and cash.

On 14 October Leven sent a final demand; less cordial in tone: An equally defiant response was returned: Leven in turn answered that he was willing to exchange hostages and parlay. Whilst Marley temporised and sent a vacillating reply he didn't close the door on negotiations. More finely nuanced correspondence ensued. Leven grew ever more frustrated at what were obviously delaying tactics. Letters passed back and forth as the two sides crept towards acceptable terms for parlay.

These negotiations required considerable finessing; who should be sent as hostages and who should be appointed commissioners? At length Colonel Charles Brandling, Lieutenant Colonel Thomas Davieson and Captain Cuthbert Carr were sent from the City. Marley, Sir Nicholas Cole and Sir George Baker with a single secretary should form the Royalists negotiating team. On 18 October, at nine in the morning, the hostages were sent out via Sandgate and the Scots commissioners came in. Leven had appointed Sir Adam Hepburn, his treasurer, Sir David Hume and John Rutherford with their own secretary.

The best that the defenders could hope for was that the onset of winter might somehow force the Scots to abandon their siege. Given the vast investment of materiel and resources this was at one level unlikely. On the other hand, sickness and desertion were eroding the ranks faster than roundshot. Battering the walls by Newgate had shown how swiftly breaches could be opened and, given the very long odds, there was no real prospect of beating off any determined assault.

Leven was demonstrably running short of patience. Winter would increase his problems tenfold. The meeting of both sets of commissioners on 18 October proved pointless. When the Scots reported to their commander, he was clearly exasperated and decided to settle the business next day by force. In the afternoon Leven *set to work against the town.* Callendar's batteries were deployed to bring fire down on the south eastern and south western flank of the town at Sandgate and Closegate respectively. Infantry battalions moved up onto the higher ground near the stream by Barras Bridge.

So thin were the ranks of the defenders that Marley ordered the evacuation of the Shieldfield fort; he needed the three hundred strong garrison to man the walls. The sconce was torched as the defenders withdrew. This evident preparation, as the Scottish general had hoped, did serve to concentrate the minds of the councillors who wrote to him that evening. Their tone was distinctly more upbeat and they asked only that he hold off till Monday by when they would get back to him with more detailed proposals.

Leven summoned an urgent council of war with his officers, no easy matter as these were widely scattered. A swift reply was drafted and sent. As ever the Scot was punctilious but spoke plainly that he would brook no more prevarication. Terms were precise and the defenders were instructed to confirm their outright surrender to Lord Sinclair's quarters by six o' clock next morning, together with more hostages.

The Scottish general's terms were pretty fair. All officers and men who wished could march out unmolested with their weapons and kit. Any citizens feeling the same way could follow; sick and infirm residents would receive full care; those who stayed should have no fear of mishandling from the Scots. All those ancient rights and privileges of the town would be guaranteed. Gentlemen who chose to discreetly retire to their country houses could do so freely. There no free quartering of Scottish troops and only a modest garrison would be installed.

Promptly, at six next morning, 19 October, the Scottish batteries boomed, targeting their shot at Sandgate, Pilgrim Street Gate, Westgate and below the White Friars Tower. The bombardment lasted for a long two hours by which time Marley's final response reached Leven.

This was not encouraging. The Mayor persisted in his earlier vacillation – he reminded Leven that it was the Scots who had demanded terms rather than the council who had offered them. He didn't refuse the summons outright but asked for a further delay till Monday 21st for a considered response. Marley went on to intimate there were further articles to be negotiated prior to any formal surrender. This intransigence came as no surprise, Hepburn confirms it was more or less what the Scots had been expecting, hence their show of firepower. In fairness to Marley, King Charles had form for executing officers who threw in the towel too easily. He had his own bets to hedge.

For the covenanters further delay was unacceptable. Winter was indeed drawing on, maintaining their siege lines was very costly and the defenders' counter-mining threatened to flood more of their galleries. Leven sent no reply and Marley wrote now to Sinclair, a rather disordered communication, suggesting Leven was somehow dead and 'wishing you could think of some other course to compose the differences of these sad distracted kingdoms, than by battering Newcastle …' Leven drily confirmed he was still drawing breath and 'hoped he might do him [Marley] some service yet before he died.'

But the time for talking was over.

Even the dour covenanting writer and eyewitness, William Lithgow, not one to go overboard with admiration, had described Newcastle's walls as formidable, more so in his opinion 'than those of York, and not unlike to the walls of Avignon, but especially of Jerusalem'. Though the city walls were strong and the castle well sited on its prominent bluff, the defences were vulnerable to bombardment on three sides, east, west and south. The Pandon Burn, to the east, cut through a valley on its course to the Tyne. This ground rose considerably and lay a mere half mile from Sandgate. Where the walls ran along the western flank of Pandon

City Walls Newcastle. (Authors own, courtesy of Adam Barr (Adamski))

Dene there was little prospect for a direct assault and, until its abandonment, these had been covered by the Shieldfield Fort.

West of the sconce stood a now-vanished windmill and, as the circuit of walls faced north, the ground offered little scope for artillerymen. Just in front of Pilgrim Street Gate, a level swell rose with a lateral ridge running from Newgate to the Leazes. Here, on the west, the wall was more fully exposed and offered a more tempting prospect. As the curtain swung down towards the river, yet more high ground from Elswick and Benwell favoured the attacker. The sharp drop towards Closegate and the riverside was less attractive but the steep bank facilitated mining operations. This fortress, notwithstanding its medieval walls, was a very difficult nut to crack.

Leven continued to rely on both guns and mines. The artillery was to punch holes in the walls at Closegate, Newgate and by Carliol Tower. Four batteries had been placed; that on the south west giving the gunners a clear field of fire.

With a total train of a hundred and twenty heavy guns, Leven wasn't short of firepower. Sandy Hamilton's newly designed and highly portable 12-pounders certainly played their part (though it would seem that the heavier 24-pounder was a favoured siege weight). Such weapons were not effective at much over a thousand yards and most devastating at around four hundred. The average distance from gun to target averaged seven to eight hundred yards – within effective shooting range.

Throughout the siege Marley's men had flooded more than half a dozen mines but a further four were blown during or just prior to the main assault. There is some disagreement as to precisely when these were fired – Lithgow states that the one beneath White Friar Tower and one of the pair at Sandgate went up at 15.00 hours and the last two a couple of hours later.

Mines, properly laid, were capable of blasting whole sections of the wall skywards, offering stunned defenders no opportunity to remedy the gaping breach. Scots gunners too did their part. More sections of masonry were collapsed at Closegate, between Andrew Tower; Newgate, between Pilgrim Street Gate; Carliol

Tower and perhaps also at Sandgate. In all Scottish mines and ordnance blasted six major gaps in the defences. With the slender resources available Marley could not hope to plug even half of these sufficiently to withstand infantry assault.

For the townspeople who would, to a degree, have become accustomed to the daily routine of bombardment and counter battery work, this must have seemed like dawn of the Apocalypse. The noise would have been terrific, like a hundred express trains charging through the streets, buildings shaking with each reverberating blast. Houses that were struck by random shot collapsed like packs of cards, burying the inhabitants. Shards of stone and lethal wood splinters spat like razors. This furious tempo would continue throughout the morning till the mines were sprung.

Now, as Scottish foot brigades formed up under arms awaiting orders, the officers cast dice, black being the desired result, to see who should command at which point. The post of maximum danger was much coveted – 'hurry to meet death lest another take your place.' Here was opportunity, probably the last as the war was seen to be winding down. If an ambitious young firebrand wanted glory the breach was where it sprouted.

The first of four *tercios* (brigades) was deployed in three lines each of two battalions, standing behind the batteries on the western flank. First into the attack here would be Loudon-Glasgow's (Lord Loudoun) and Tweeddale's (Scott of Buccleuch) regiments, both led by their colonels, storming the breach at Closegate. Next, the Clydesdale (Sandy Hamilton, General of Artillery) and Edinburgh men (James Rae) would attempt to force a way in by the gap blown by the mine below White Friar Tower. Lastly, the men of Galloway (William Stewart) and Perthshire (Lord Gask) would assault Westgate.

Moving north towards the Newgate a second tercio waited. Baillie, as CO, would lead the Angus men, Strathearn's (Lord Cowper), Fife (Lord Dunfermline), East Lothian (Sir Patrick Hepburn) and one other unmanned regiment. Baillie's tercio was the most powerful, a tribute to the strength of Newgate. Opposite

Pilgrim Street Gate stood the regiments of Kyle & Carrick (Lord Cassillis), Nithsdale & Annandale (Douglas of Kilhead), Mearns and Aberdeen (the Earl Marischall), Linlithgow & Tweeddale (Master of Yester), and finally the Merse Battalion (Sir David Hume of Wedderburn). Callendar had the fourth tercio in hand at Sandgate comprising Lord Sinclair's Levies, the Stirling men (Lord Livingstone), bolstered by strong companies or rather ad hoc units under Sir John Aytoun, Sir John Wauchope of Niddrie and the Master of Cranstoun. In reserve were most probably the Midlothian, Teviotdale and Ministers' Regiments.

Professor Terry has provided a detailed analysis of the strength of the Scottish attacking force. This is based upon a total of 140 companies at an average of 90 soldiers per company, reflecting the stated strength of the infantry in January 1644 as 18,000. We support Stuart Reid's more modern estimation and, allowing for casualties, sick and deserters (clearly a major problem), we would suggest that the average company strength was no greater than 50. This provides a total of 7,000 men in the attack, rather than 12,600 which Terry suggests.

The same reasoning must be applied to Callendar's division which had, of course, seen less campaigning. Numerous units were stationed in outposts and Terry assesses Callendar's total strength at around 3,000. We see no compelling reason to dispute this. What is clear is that these men took no direct part in the assault on 19 October, they formed a strategic reserve and provided infantry cover for those batteries on the Gateshead side.

Nonetheless, the defenders were massively outnumbered, even allowing for the authors' slashing of totals. Lithgow affirms 'they were but eight hundred of the Trained Band, and some nine hundred besides, of volunteers, pressed men [conscripts], colliers, keel-men and poor tradesmen; with some few experimented [experienced] officers to overtop [command] them.' Tantalisingly few details of how these meagre forces were deployed have survived. Cuthbert Carr may have commanded at Newgate. Captain George Errington, Lieutenant William Robson and Thomas Swan held Pilgrim Gate with 180 chosen men.

At both points the defenders fought with great courage, holding on even when the defence generally had collapsed, sallying out from time to time to beat back the tide. Errington's men (who amazingly suffered no serious loss) even fired upon those of their friends who later called upon them to strike their colours! We know that John Marley with a body of diehards fell back into the castle and its improvised outworks when the rest were overrun.

Lithgow does provide a gritty account of the nature of the assault:

> so also I say the breaches of the walls by batteries, being made open and passable, and ladders set to at diverse parts for scalleting [scaling], then entered mainely and manfully all the regiments of our commanded men at all quarters, but more facily [easily] and less dangerous where the mines sprung. The greatest difficulty and mightiest opposition, nay, and the sorest slaughter we received was at the climbing up of these steep and stay breaches, where truly, and too truly, the enemy did more harm with hand grenades than either with musket pike or Herculean clubs.

These clubs were anti-personnel weapons devised for just such work, like long, heavy version of a medieval spiked mace 'it grimly looked like to the pale face of murther [murder]'.

As the fight came to 'push of pike', men stumbled and scrambled to come to grips on blood slicked stone; hacking and clawing at each-other, consumed by the adrenalin rush 'red mist' of combat. As the Scots fought their way into Closegate, Royalist cavalry mounted three desperate charges trying to push them back, but cavalry couldn't fight pikes and regular volleys in such a confined space. From here, as the official account confirms the attackers 'marched for the relief of the rest of the breaches, and so the soldiers gave over and forsook the walls'.

With the Scots established within the ring, the walls were no longer tenable and men fled back into the town, apart from those bastions like Newgate and Pilgrim Gate which doggedly clung on. Surprisingly perhaps the Scots did not then have to fight for possession of a warren of streets and lanes: 'for after their entry, the soldiers did quite vanish, sheltering themselves in houses, the inhabitants kept closed their doors, the regiments marched through the streets without any insolence or disorder'. The Scottish commander is at pains to stress that his men behaved impeccably with a strict avoidance of pillage and offering no violence to citizens not under arms. Once the attackers had punched through, then bodies of infantry would be told off from the columns to secure the streets.

Leven in his report makes the point that, as the town had refused terms and been taken at sword-point, the Scots were at liberty to sack the place. That they did not reflects well upon standards of discipline. The general does allow that some 'little pillage' did occur, mainly directed against 'some houses of the meaner sort'. Robbing the poor was clearly less reprehensible than pilfering the rich! Leven goes on to wax lyrical over his own virtue and moderation. Why not, he'd won?

As his reserve regiments followed the successful assault, Callendar sent the Nithsdale and Annandale men to clear the eastern flank of the town. Lithgow tells us that although some defenders simply disappeared into their own or other's houses, there was a final stand by the more determined in the Cloth Market. There, caught between twin pincers, survivors laid down their arms and begged for quarter. Consolidation by the Scots was perhaps less orderly than Leven's rather smug dispatch claims. Lithgow asserts there was some indiscipline and looting, doubly shocking to his Calvinist sensibilities.

Meanwhile, back in the castle, Marley had run up a flag of truce which the Scots ignored – the Mayor had delayed rather too long. His next letter to Leven was couched in rather less bombastic terms. He asked that what was left of the garrison should be offered the same terms as before and allowed free passage. That was not going to happen.

For the next three days autumnal gales battered both winners and losers, sweeping aside pontoon bridges. Before the storms had abated Sir John and the other survivors had surrendered unconditionally.

The Mayor was placed under house arrest; with a strong guard, not to keep him in but to keep the vengeful mob out. When taken from his home to a less congenial billet in the cells, Marley was roughed up a bit and, when he was committed to the custody of Sheriff Whalton, the mob was baying for his blood. In fact Marley not only survived but contrived to escape or was allowed to slip away into exile abroad. He would return with Charles II. When last heard of, he was a Member of Parliament sitting on a commission looking into MP's expenses. Unsurprisingly, the commission voted for an increase.

Kate o' Harnham

Now Harnham Hall is a wonderful place. It was fortified, described as a 'fortalice' in 1415, though it looks more like a prime setting for *Wuthering Heights*. It stands, remote, on a set of steep-sided bluffs. Most of what remains dates from the 17th and 18th centuries, though traces of medieval stonework do survive. A recent owner used to offer an explanation for what appears to be rampant woodworm in the wainscoting of the hallway but is in damage caused by shotgun pellets. His father at the turn of the 20th century, when in drink, which was often, used to think he saw the devil prancing on the stairs and took appropriate action!

The drawing room ceiling bears a great flaming dragon in plaster, crest of the Babington's who owned the place from 1660–1667. Katherine or Kate Babington was a daughter of leading parliamentarian, Sir Arthur Hazelrigg. He had raised a cavalry regiment nicknamed the lobsters on account of the heavy armour they carried, though this hadn't stopped them running away at Roundway (Runaway) Down. Kate was every bit as contentious as her father, blessed with astonishing looks. Her contemporaries reckoned her the most beautiful woman in England.

Philip Babington was her second husband (the first, Colonel George Fenwick died relatively young). Babington had a good war and was made governor of Berwick for a time. Kate's parliamentarian connections were rock solid and she and Philip were the Posh and Becks of their day. She was such a celeb whole towns ground to a halt when she passed through, crowds surged to get a glimpse of such astonishing looks.

The spectacle of Kate eating a pie in public in Durham so obsessed the scholars new byelaws had to be passed to prevent the young from being so corrupted. She was not enamoured of the established church nor was the Reverend Forster of Bolam much enamoured of Kate. A high church Anglican, Kate was frequently a target for pulpit bile. One of her legion of admirers, a sturdy local blacksmith, either of his own volition or after some gentle encouragement, assaulted the vitriolic vicar, dragged him from his own lectern and threw him into the local pond.

Dour Forster did not forgive and forget. When King Charles II came back in 1660 the established church recovered its hegemony. He was still in holy orders ten years later when Kate died (still probably only in her mid-thirties). He had earlier excommunicated her (and her blacksmith) and refused to have her buried in consecrated ground. Babington built her a tomb, cut from the crag in the terraced garden of the main house. Her remains are long gone but the funerary inscription survives: 'My time is past as you may see/ I've viewed the dead as you do me/ Or long you'll lie as low as I/ And some will look on thee.'

CHAPTER 8

NOW A GENTLEMAN'S RESIDENCE

IN EARLY SEPTEMBER 2014, Barack Obama and a whole gallery of world leaders were photographed in front of Cardiff Castle, a glittering array of power brokers assembled for a NATO summit. It was wonderful theatre choreographed by Britain's then Prime Minister David Cameron. The extravagant backdrop of the castle provided a marvellous set.

Spectacle, a capacity to dazzle, has always been a feature of castle architecture; there's nothing new about blinging it up. The need to overawe, to impress, even to intimidate was a specific aim. Late medieval castles like Bodiam were primarily intended to show off the ostentatious wealth of their newly wealthy owners.

Cardiff does have a good pedigree – some of it is even original. The Romans built a fort there in the 3rd century AD and Norman invaders later threw up a classic motte. The castle dominated the bustling medieval settlement, possibly even ordered by Duke William himself. In the 12th century Robert of Gloucester, a great Marcher lord, rebuilt in stone with a shell keep. The sixth earl added new defences later that century, not just for show. The place was regularly on the front line in the conflict between Welsh and English and was assailed by Owain Glyndwr in 1404. It changed hands in the Civil Wars and was lucky to escape Cromwell's wrecking crew.

In the mid-18th century the place passed into the hands of John Stuart, Marquess of Bute. He brought in Henry Holland and Capability Brown to give the bailey a top end Georgian makeover. A lot of the medieval was casually swept away in a wave of brash, assertive modernity. The Butes could afford it; their wealth was based not on blood but on sweat: mainly that of others. Coal had made them very rich indeed, with the wherewithal to fund a fresh makeover. The Marquess took it back to the Gothic, or at least a dazzling Victorian pastiche of it. He brought in architect William Burges and gave him a blank cheque.

No expense was spared, no detail overlooked. The new fad for archaeology and antiquity, fuelled by the excavation of Roman remains in Europe, was enough to merit the building of a new imperial style gateway. It is a gargantuan example of a rich man's folly but saved by extraordinary craftsmanship and sheer bravado. It's not a castle in the classic sense, for it was never intended to be defended. But Master James might, we think, have approved.

Work continued into the 20th century but the Depression, and Hitler eroded the fantasy. During World War Two it was relegated to a role as a large air raid shelter and sold off in the drab post war epoch of austerity. A fresh round of civic investment has restored the castle as a heritage, tourism and museum centre, like so many of Edward I Welsh castles.

Gothic was all the rage, encouraged by the work of Walter Scott. His wonderful romantic novels, *Ivanhoe* especially, were all-time best sellers. These and his re-discovery of Scotland changed the face of British castles. The Northern kingdom, since the final defeat of the Jacobites in 1746, had become the intellectual powerhouse of Europe. As Robert Adam raised the Georgian elegance of the New Town in Edinburgh, Scottish thinkers spearheaded the Enlightenment.

Wealth of empire and industry flowed into gentlemen's coffers. That largesse was not evenly distributed. Huge armies of workers laboured, often under dreadful conditions, to pay for it all. They allowed the wealthy to indulge their literary-fuelled fantasies. Scott himself did a pretty good job at Abbotsford. Medieval piles like Alnwick and Bamburgh got the full treatment, out with the Grecian, in with the Gothic.

Lord Armstrong, the 19th-century Tyneside industrial magnate who acquired Bamburgh also built himself a country house in a wonderful setting near Rothbury. It is not a castle, but his intent was just the same. It was one of the first properties to enjoy electricity and, above all, it's built to impress. Anyone who came to Cragside would be immediately aware of how successful Armstrong had been in creating his fortune.

It sets Armstrong's brand on the landscape. Quite literally. West of the house, in woods, a boundary stone marks the line between his land and the Duke of Northumberland's. On one side is a capital 'N' for the ancient line of Percies and on the other, the letter 'A'. There were some ready to suggest that the latter actually stood for '*arriviste*'.

Cardiff was not the only site to benefit from the Third Marquess' largesse. Not far outside the city another Norman motte was thrown up near the village of Tongwynlais covering the Taff Gorge. In the 13th century the site of Castell Coch, which had earlier been abandoned, was rebuilt in stone by Gilbert de Clare, another of those Marcher lords. De Clare had spotted its strategic importance, commanding both the plains area and the entrance to the Taff valley. The rebuild was in stone – Julius Caesar Ibbetson's painting of the ruins indicates that it consisted of a keep, towers, an enclosed courtyard and a gatehouse.

It appears to have been slighted during the conflict of the early 14th century. Certainly, in Tudor times, John Leyland described it as 'al in ruine'. Bute inherited Castell Coch (Red Castle in Welsh) in 1848 and hired Burges to carry out suitable and expensive renovations in 1871. Burges and the Marquess had, by that time, been working for over three years on their Cardiff project. Here they aimed for a gothic revival done in 13th-century style.

Burges has left us his plans, together with a detailed exposition of his thinking. The most picturesque, and archaeologically questionable, features of the reconstruction are the three conical roofs to the towers. Burges loved them for their visual

Castell Coch. (Andy Dingley, Wikimedia Commons, CC BY-SA 3.0)

effect, admitting that they were 'utterly conjectural' but 'more picturesque and ... affording much more accommodation'. He argued that there was some evidence for their accuracy:

> It is true that some antiquaries deny the existence of high roofs in English Mediaeval Military Architecture, and ask objectors to point out examples. As nearly every Castle in the country has been ruined for more than two centuries…it is not surprising that no examples are to be found. But we may form a very fair idea of the case if we consult contemporary (manuscripts) and if we do we find nearly an equal number of towers with flat roofs as those with pointed roofs. The case appears to me to be thus: if a tower presented a good situation for military engines, it had a flat top; if the contrary; it had a high roof to guarantee the defenders from the rain and the lighter sorts of missiles. Thus an arrow could not pierce the roof, but if the latter were absent and the arrow was fired upright, in its downward flight it might occasion the same accident to the defenders as happened to Harold at Hastings.

The three towers, the keep, the well tower and the kitchen tower, incorporate a sumptuous series of apartments; of which the main sequence, the castellan's rooms, lie within the keep. The hall, the drawing room, Lord Bute's bedroom and Lady Bute's bedroom are gorgeous, epic High Victorian Gothic style.

Building work had been completed by 1881 when Burges met an untimely death. An enormous amount remained to be done internally and worked continued for another decade. The later work does not show the same skill and flair though it is very fine.

This aside, the drawing room and Lady Bute's bedroom are fantastical creations with an exuberance that overpowers the visitor. The ceilings and wall paintings are dazzling in their richness and fully equal the best achieved at Cardiff Castle. In addition, the exterior of the castle is an awesome display of architectural power and ability. In a lecture, Burges called on architectural students to 'study the great broad masses, the strong un-chamfered lines'. He had clearly done so: the combinations of cone, square and drum which he achieved at Castell Coch demonstrate his architectural mastery.

Oddly, the castle had not been intended to function as a permanent residence and the family's visits were infrequent (although the marchioness and her daughter did live there for a short period following her husband's death in 1900). In 1950, the 5th Marquess of Bute placed the castle in the care of the Ministry of Works. It is now administered by CADW on behalf of the National Assembly for Wales.

It is breathtaking; the very model of a medieval baronial castle. Far more stylish than its Cardiff counterpart, it has been described as 'one of the greatest Victorian triumphs of architectural composition'. It is.

We want it to be the real thing, this perfect imagined castle. Straight out of Malory or Tennyson, superbly located, elevated and wooded, it's the enchanted castle of our dreams. There are plenty of originals in Brittany or Burgundy that look just like it. It demands mailed horsemen riding out through the gate with a feisty female castellan watching from high windows and thinking thoughts no troubadour would have approved of.

In North Northumberland on magical Holy Island, a landscape that drips history and romance stands another perfect castle, the epitome of a fantasy medieval fortress, the kind you would expect to find in a Hollywood movie. Like Castell Coch, the present reality is a late reconstruction of a projected past.

Built on a dolerite outcrop, there has been a citadel on the site since the 5th century and was for many years the capital of an Anglo-Saxon kingdom. The Vikings destroyed the original fortification in 993.

Bamburgh may have been the stronghold of the rebel leader – Gospatrick, Earl of Northumbria – whose actions prompted William the Conqueror to venture north to snuff out resistance in 1068. It cost Gospatrick his earldom, passed to the more reliable figure of William Walcher, Bishop of Durham. It was either William I or Walcher who established the first castle on the site. The Normans built a new castle on the site, which forms the core of the present one. They built well, it was well able to withstand its first siege just a few years' later.

In 1086 Bamburgh was granted to Robert de Mowbray, Earl of Northumberland. Robert used the castle as a base to secure

Bamburgh Castle. (Michael Hanselmann, Wikimedia Commons, CC BY-SA 3.0)

the north against Scottish incursions and deployed from the castle to engage the Scots at the First Battle of Alnwick in 1093, killing the Scots king.

In 1095 Mowbray took part in a rebellion aimed at replacing William Rufus with his cousin, Stephen of Aumale. Robert showed poor judgement: most of his fellow conspirators abandoned the plot leaving Mowbray and his fellow plotters (including William of Eu) exposed.

Everything fell apart when Mowbray seized four Norwegian vessels lying in the Tyne. The owners complained to the king and Mowbray was commanded to attend the Curia Regis to explain his actions. He ignored the summons, a rash move when dealing with a man of William II's temper.

Mowbray shut himself up in his stronghold at Bamburgh and prepared to sit it out as William threw up a temporary siege castle alongside it, known as a Malvoisin, or "evil neighbour". Yet again, his poor judgement proved his undoing. Abandoning his wife who took over command, he fled with a small force of knights, hotly pursued by William. Once again besieged, this time in Tynemouth, he managed to hold out for all of six days. The wounded man was hauled back to Bamburgh to be used in cajoling the surrender of the capable Matilda.

Fortunately for Robert, she was rather more perceptive. William's threat to blind and castrate her husband was a potent one. Matilda showed good sense in handing over the castle. William would have followed through on his promise – it was precisely what happened to Roberts's co-conspirator, William of Eu.

Mowbray forfeited his estates and was imprisoned for life, initially at Windsor Castle. He spent many years in prisons, 'growing old without offspring', according to Florence of Worcester, before being allowed to become a monk at St Albans Abbey.

He must have hated it. Orderic Vitalis gives us a description of Robert de Mowbray at the height of his powers. 'Powerful, rich, bold, fierce in war, haughty, he despised his equals and, swollen with vanity, disdained to obey his superiors. He was of great stature, strong, swarthy and hairy. Daring and crafty, stern and grim, he was given more to meditation than speech, and in conversation scarce ever smiled.' Well, at least he was fitted for silent contemplation.

Matilda had clearly had enough. She sought an annulment of her marriage and, sometime after 1107; she married Robert's brother Nigel d'Aubigny, who was granted some of the lands forfeited by her former husband.

Siege works like the Malvoisin were erected when speed was of the essence to reduce the defence. Historians argue whether they were a combined earthen embankment with a fronting ditch thrown up to protect the besiegers or a timber siege tower (or belfry). In later years the term would also be used of siege engines such as the trebuchet used against Prince Louis. The answer seems to be that all three apply.

The earthen structure was both defensive and offensive providing shelter for the aggressors and a platform to get close to the castle whilst staying just out of firing range. Their use was, by definition, temporary so few remain. One exception are the mighty ring-works at Corfe Castle in Devon, erected by King Stephen in 1189. They are still visible from the air.

Bamburgh Castle now became the property of Eustace Fitz John who initiated rebuilding the structure in stone. It withstood an attack by the Scots in December 1135 but, the situation was not to last. Anxious to avoid fighting on two fronts King Stephen handed the fortress over to the Scots in an effort at appeasement. He had enough to do fighting it out with his cousin, another Matilda. It may have been Prince Henry of Scotland who launched the construction of the great keep.

It may have been Henry who commenced construction of the Great Keep but its completion was the work of another Henry: this time an English one. Henry II took back control of northern England in 1157. Bamburgh became the property of the reigning English monarch. As an important English outpost, the castle was the target of occasional raids from Scotland.

In 1333, whilst Edward III was besieging Berwick-upon-Tweed, Queen Philippa stayed at Bamburgh. Hoping to lure

Edward away, the Scots laid siege to her. Edward did not fall for it. He was confident the defences would hold and remained in situ. The Scots were forced to withdraw. Following the Battle of Neville's Cross was deemed strong enough to serve as a prison for King David II of Scotland.

After the Wars of the Roses, the property passed into the hands of the church; only to be forcibly wrested from them by Henry VIII in 1545. Like so many ecclesiastical properties caught up in the dissolution, it was swiftly sold at cut price rates to a local man in this case, Sir John Forster. Who paid all of £664 for the place.

That was fairly typical of Forster who had an eye for a bargain and the capacity to make the most of it. He was probably the most notorious of the March Wardens of the 16th century, a man who was as likely to organise a reiver raid as punish one. His family had provided the Crown with twelve successive governors of the castle for some 400 years so perhaps he felt entitled. Certainly, there does not seem to have been any great affection for the place. The Forsters preferred to live at Bamburgh Hall and allowed the Castle to decay over the succeeding decades.

The family retained ownership until 1700 when Sir William Forster was posthumously declared bankrupt, and his estates, including the castle, were sold to Lord Crew, Bishop of Durham (husband of his sister Dorothy) under an Act of Parliament to settle the debts.

The castle continued remained neglected until attempts at restoration were made by various owners during the 18th and 19th centuries. It was finally bought in 1894 by the Victorian industrialist William Armstrong, the same man who created Cragside. He immediately set to work restoring it: another great project to entertain his later years.

It would not be until the turn of the 20th century, when publishing entrepreneur and tycoon Edward Hudson, owner of *Country Life* bought the ruin that it would finally emerge as remarkable structure we see today. Hudson promptly hired the architect, Edwin Lutyens to carry out a complete makeover.

Bamburgh Castle from the beach. (Author's own, courtesy of Adam Barr (Adamski))

Sir Edwin did a very fine job, creating a diminutive country house/castle which dominates the archipelago as though straight out of a fairytale romance. It is truly beautiful, all in proportion and set in a wild, harsh seascape that shifts and changes with the restless tide. Filmmakers love it, Roman Polanski made *Cul de Sac* and then *Macbeth* there (John was an extra in that). It even appears in a version of *the Scarlet Pimpernel* with Anthony Andrews.

May 2017 – *The Daily Mail* marvelled at the flat available to rent in what remains of the oldest part of the structure – the Keep, a mere £300 per week. Bamburgh is renowned for its clean air, a positive draw for the asthmatic and bronchially afflicted. Armstrong was not the first to notice this but he was the first to spot its medical potential. He had suggested that, after his death, the castle be used as a convalescent home: the strong onshore winds either killing or curing the patients.

These were not the only castles to have a modern reincarnation. Near Treigny in Burgundy a team of enthusiasts and experts are building a 13th-century knightly castle from scratch. Begun in 1997 by castle-owner Michel Guyot it's a generational project and won't be complete for several years yet. It's a brilliant fusion of experimental archaeology, heritage tourism and sheer, glorious anorak enthusiasm. All the techniques, tools and gear being used are traditional. Stones are quarried and cut locally; it's a perfect expression of experimental archaeology in action. The learning and discovery curve is steep but the skill, dedication, commitment and sheer *joie* are magnificent. Guedelon is as near to the original as we'll ever come, another jewel waiting to be enjoyed.

The castle story is not ended just yet.

The Ghostly Bridal

Featherstone Castle stands in the west of Northumberland, not far from the market town of Haltwhistle. It has a fine setting. The extended tower house covers the confluence of the Hartley Burn and North Tyne, described by a 19th-century writer, the splendidly named Cadwallader Bates, who restored nearby Langley, as 'loveliest in the country'. The core dates from the early 13th century but it was given a substantial makeover in the 19th and the family seem originally to have been called Featherstone-Haugh.

On 24 October 1530, Albany Featherstone-Haugh, then serving as High Sheriff, was gunned down by the Ridleys less than a mile from his front door. The feud between the two families went back several generations.

His daughter, Abigail fell for one of the Ridleys. The attraction was mutual but her father would have none of it. He had a far more suitable match in mind – she was to marry a distant and well-heeled cousin. It seems Abigail wasn't consulted.

Family custom had it that, once the ceremony was over and before the wedding breakfast, the bridal party changed into hunting kit and did a mounted tour of the estate. We don't know how large the group was but there must have been a decent number. As they trotted round the bounds they came to a narrow defile, the Pinkyn Cleugh. Here young Ridley and his gang staged an ambush. It may well be Abigail was party to the plan.

The whole thing went pretty badly wrong. This being Northumberland, the wedding party were naturally well-armed and nobody minded a scrap before dinner. It got very messy. Ridley was nearly felled by his rival but Abigail bravely, if unwisely, took the blow and died. Ridley did for the husband then killed himself out of remorse. Nobody else survived on either side.

Meanwhile the baron himself was supervising the loading of his groaning trestles. He waited all afternoon and long into the dusk. Still sitting there at midnight he was treated to a silent and terrible procession of the newly weds and all their bright guests, spectres all, pale and ghastly, gliding silently through the furniture. They say the dreadful sight sent him mad. That is how the servants found him next day.

BIBLIOGRAPHY

Bain, J. (ed.), *Calendar of Documents Relating to Scotland 1108–1509* (1881–1884)

Barbour, R., *The Knight and Chivalry* (London 1974)

Bartlett, C., *The English Longbowman 1313–1515* (England 1995)

Bates, C. J., *History of Northumberland* (London 1895)

Bradbury, J., *the Medieval Siege* (Woodbridge 1992)

Brown, R. A., *English Castles* (3rd Edition, London 1976)

Brown R. A., H. M. Colvin & A. J. Taylor (ed.), *History of the King's Works* (in six volumes, London 1963)

Cathcart King, D. J., *Castellarium Anglicanum* volume 2 (New York 1983)

Charlesworth, D., *Northumberland in the Early Years of Edward 1V* in 'Archaeologia Aeliana' (4th Series 1953)

Child, F. J., *The English and Scottish Popular Ballads* (New York, 1965), volume 1

Colvin, H. M., D. R. Ransome & J. Summerson, *History of the King's Works* III 1485–1660 Part 1

Coventry, M., *The Castles of Scotland* (3rd edition, Mussleburgh 2001)

Crow, J., *Harbottle Castle, Excavations and Survey 1997–1999* in 'Archaeology in Northumberland National Park'

Hartshorne, C. H., *Memoirs Illustrative of the History and Antiquities of Northumberland* volume 2, 'Feudal and Military Antiquities of Northumberland and the Scottish Borders' (London 1852)

Haythornthwaite, P., *The English Civil War 1642–1651* (London, 1994)

Hepple, L. W., *A History of Northumberland and Newcastle upon Tyne* (London 1976).

Higham, R. & P. Barker, *Timber Castles* (London, 1992)

Hodgson, *Northumberland* Part II volume 1

Hope Dodds M. (editor), *A History of Northumberland* volume 15 (Newcastle upon Tyne 1940)

Hugill, R., *Castles and Peles of the English Border* (Newcastle 1970)

Hunter Blair, C.H., *Harbottle Castle* in 'History of the Berwickshire Naturalists Club' xxviii (1932–1934)

Johnson, M., *Behind the Castle Gate: From Medieval to Renaissance* (London 2002)

Keen, M. (ed.) *Medieval Warfare – a History* (Oxford 1999)

Kightly J., *Flodden and the Anglo-Scottish war 1513* (London, 1975)

Lang, J., *Stories of the Border Marches* (New York, 1916)

Leadman, A. D., *The Battle of Towton*, Yorkshire Archaeological Journal vol. 10 (1889)

Lomas, R., *Northumberland – County of Conflict* (East Lothian 1996)

Lomas, R., *North-East England in The Middle Ages* (Edinburgh 1992)

Long, B., *The Castles of Northumberland* (Newcastle upon Tyne 1967)

Lynch, M., *A New History of Scotland* (London 1991)

Macdonald-Fraser, G., The Steel Bonnets (London, 1971)

Macdougall, N., *James III: A Political Study* (Edinburgh 1982)

MacGibbon & T. Ross, *The castellated and Domestic Architecture of Scotland from the Twelfth to the Eighteenth Century* (in five volumes, Edinburgh 1887 – 1892)

Morris, M., *Castle; a History of the Buildings that Shaped Medieval Britain* (London, 2012)

Neillands, R., *The Hundred Years War* (London 1990)

Neillands, R., *The Wars of the Roses* (London 1992)

Nicolle, D., *Medieval Warfare Source Book* (London 1999)

Norman, A. V. B. and D. Pottinger, *English Weapons and Warfare 449 – 1660* (London 1966)

Percy Hedley, W., *Northumberland Families* vol. 1 (Society of Antiquaries of Newcastle upon Tyne, 1968)

Pevsner, N. & I. Richmond, *Northumberland* in 'The Buildings of England' Series (London 1992)

Phillips, G., *The Anglo-Scots Wars 1513–1550* (Woodbridge, 1999)

Pollard, A. J., '*Percies, Nevilles and the Wars of the Roses*' in *History Today* (September 1992)

Pollard, A. J., *The Wars of the Roses* (England 1995)

Pollard, A. J., *North-eastern England during the Wars of the Roses: War, Politics and Lay Society, 1450–1500* (Oxford 1990)

Prestwich, M., *Armies and Warfare in the Middle Ages* (London 1996)

Proceedings of the Society of Antiquaries of Newcastle upon Tyne (volume IX)

Ridpath, G., *The Border History of England and Scotland* (Berwick upon Tweed 1776)

Robson, R., *Rise and Fall of the English Highland Clans: Tudor Responses to a Medieval Problem* (Edinburgh, 1997)

Rogers, Col. H. C. B., *Artillery Through the Ages* (London 1971)

Royal Commission on Historic Monuments *Shielings and Bastles* (HMSO, 1970)

Ryder, P. F., *Harbottle castle – a short historical and descriptive account* (February 1990)

Sadler, D. J., *Battle for Northumbria* (England 1988)

Sadler, D. J., *War in the North – The Wars of the Roses in the North East of England 1461–1464* (England 2000)

Sadler, D. J., *Border Fury – The Three Hundred Years War* (England 2004)

Sadler D. J., & R. Serdiville *The Battle of Flodden 1513* (Stroud, 2013)

Scott, Sir Walter, *Minstrelsy (*London, 1892 edition*)*

Storey, R. L., 'The Wardens of the Marches of England towards Scotland 1377–1489', *English Historical Review* (72: 1957)

Summerson, H., 'Carlisle and the English West March in the Late Middle Ages' in *The North of England in the Reign of Richard III* (England 1996)

Tabraham, C., *Scotland's Castles* (London 1997)

Taylor, A., *Studies in Castles and Castle Building* (London 1985)

Thompson, M. W., *The Rise of the Castle* (Cambridge 1987)

Thompson, M. W., *The Decline of the Castle* (Cambridge 1987)

Tough, D. L. W., *The Last Years of a Frontier* (Oxford 1928)

Warner, P., *Sieges of the Middle Ages* (London 1968)

ACKNOWLEDGEMENTS

This book could not have been written without the assistance and support of Chris Jones and colleagues at Northumberland National Park Authority, The National Archives, Newcastle upon Tyne City Library, the Lit and Phil Library, the Library of the Society of Antiquaries of Newcastle upon Tyne, the Durham Palatine Archives, Tyne and Wear and Northumberland Archives, staff at Alnwick Castle, English Heritage, The National Trust, Historic Scotland and the National Trust for Scotland. We are also indebted to Peter Ryder, George and John Common, Aidan Pratt, Margaret Mitchinson, Beryl Charlton, the late David Winston, the late Alec Bankier, the late Professor George Jobey, the late John Wake and to Silvie Fisch for the photos. And, of course to Claire Litt and the team at Casemate for yet another successful collaboration. Any errors or omissions are entirely our own.

Rosie Serdiville and John Sadler,
Northumberland,
Spring 2018

INDEX